English Colonial Treaties
with the
American Indians

D1528402

AMS PRESS
NEW YORK

AN ACCOUNT

OF THE

TREATY

BETWEEN

His Excellency

Benjamin Fletcher Captain General and Governour in Chief of the Province of *New-York*, &c.

AND THE

INDIANS

OF THE

Five Nations,

VIZ.

The Mohaques, Oneydes, Onnondages, Cajonges
and Sennekes, at *Albany*, beginning the 15th of
August, 1694.

Printed & Sold by William Bradford, *Printer to Their Majesties,*
King William *and Queen* Mary, *at the Sign of the Bible in*
New-York, 1694.

FACSIMILE TITLE OF No. 3

A BIBLIOGRAPHY
OF THE
ENGLISH COLONIAL TREATIES
WITH THE AMERICAN INDIANS
INCLUDING
A SYNOPSIS OF EACH TREATY

BY

HENRY F. DE PUY

NEW YORK
PRINTED FOR THE LENOX CLUB
1917

Reprinted from the edition of 1917, New York
First AMS edition published 1971

Manufactured in the United States of America

International Standard Book Number: 0-404-07123-6

Library of Congress Card Catalogue: 78-164820

AMS PRESS INC.
NEW YORK, N.Y. 10003

INTRODUCTION

During the long period in which Great Britain and France struggled for the supremacy on the North American continent the affairs and friendship of the Indians were of the greatest importance. This was especially true of the Iroquois and the Western Indians. In New England the settlers early became the masters except of the eastern tribes of Abenakis and their kindred. The French working through their missionaries persuaded part of the Abenakis to migrate to Canada and through them exerted much influence with those who still remained in territory claimed by the English. Numerous treaties were made between these Indians and the Governors of Massachusetts Bay; and while many of the details in the treaties that were printed seem to relate only to trade, the real object of the English was to retain the Indian friendship.

The Iroquois played a more important part than the Eastern Indians and finally came to be regarded by the British colonies as a "buffer state" between them and the French. The Iroquois were well aware of their importance to both sides and the treaties with them show what astute politicians they were.

Many of the records of the various treaties with the Indians exist only in manuscript; some have been printed in the Journals of the Governors and Councils or in the "Votes and Proceedings" of the legislative bodies; while others were separately printed. It is the object of this monograph to locate and describe such as were separately printed. A very brief synopsis of the contents of each treaty is given, and also the location of copies in the principal libraries and private collections. It is quite probable that they were printed in very small editions, which would account for their rarity at the present time. That they are rare is demonstrated by the fact that only one public library in the country contains one-third of the number of titles recorded in this monograph, while thirteen titles are known by only a single copy. And of two no copy is known to exist in America. To see the ones described it has been necessary to visit the various libraries in Boston, Worcester, New York, Philadelphia, and Chicago. Seventeen public libraries and seven private collections have been examined and the copies located in them are recorded herein.

These treaties are original sources of information of some of the most important events connected with the settlement of the country and its land titles. This is especially true of the period covered by the "Old French War," for it was during that period that the northern colonies courted the Indians as a protection against the French. Many pages in them refer to the negotiations for the return of white captives among the savages. So full are they of interesting historic details that the tendency in making the synopses in this book was to extend them too far. The synopses are intended to give only a hint as to the main subjects discussed in the treaties.

Finally, the excuse for printing this work at all is the belief of the compiler that, to the special student, the most useful bibliography is the monograph on a special subject, which can give an idea of the contents of the books described, as well as their size and location.

LIST OF ENGLISH COLONIAL TREATIES

DATE OF TREATY	HELD AT	IMPRINT	
1677	Virginia	London	1677
1690	Albany	Boston	1690
1694	Albany	New York	1694
1696	Albany	New York	1696
1698	Albany	New York	1698
1717	Georgetown	Boston	1717
1721	Conestoga	Philadelphia	1721
1721	Conestoga	London	
1721	Conestoga	Dublin	1723
1722	Albany	Dublin	1723
1722	Conestoga	Philadelphia	1722
1726	Falmouth	Boston	1726
1727	Falmouth	Boston	1727
1726–7	Falmouth	Boston	1754
1728	Conestoga	Philadelphia	1728
1732	Falmouth	Boston	1732
1732	Falmouth	London	173:
1735	Deerfield	Boston	1735
1736	Philadelphia	Philadelphia	1737
1742	Philadelphia	Philadelphia	1743
1742	Philadelphia	London	1743
1742	St. Georges	Boston	1742
1743	Connecticut	London	1769
1744	Lancaster	Philadelphia	1744

DATE OF TREATY	HELD AT	IMPRINT	
1744	Lancaster	Williamsburg	
1745	Albany	Philadelphia	1746
1746	Albany	New York	1746
1747	Philadelphia	Philadelphia	1748
1748	Lancaster	Philadelphia	1748
1749	Falmouth	Boston	1749
1752	St. Georges	Boston	1752
1752	Halifax	Halifax	1752
1753	Carlisle	Philadelphia	1753
1753	St. Georges	Boston	1753
1754	Falmouth	Boston	1754
1755-6	Ft. Johnson	London	1756
1756	Crosswicks	Philadelphia	1756
1756	Catawba	Williamsburg	1756
1756	Philadelphia	Newcastle	1756
1756	Ft. Johnson	New York	1757
1756	Easton	Philadelphia	1757
1757	Harris Ferry	Philadelphia	1757
1757	Ft. Johnson	New York	1757
1757	Ft. Johnson	Boston	1757
1757	Easton	Philadelphia	1757
1758	Burlington	[Philadelphia	1758]
1758	Easton	Philadelphia	1758
1758	Easton	Philadelphia	1759
1758	Easton	Woodbridge	1758
1761	Easton	Philadelphia	1761
1762	Lancaster	Philadelphia	1763
1763	Augusta	Charleston	1764
1765	Johnson Hall	Philadelphia	1776
1768	Ft. Pitt	Philadelphia	1769

ABBREVIATIONS.

AAS.	American Antiquarian Society, Worcester.
APS.	American Philosophical Society, Philadelphia.
BA.	Boston Athenæum, Boston.
BM.	British Museum, London, England.
BPL.	Boston Public Library, Boston,
CPC.	Curtis Publishing Co., Philadelphia.
D.	Henry F. DePuy, New York.
Friend.	Friend's Library, Philadelphia.
HC.	Harvard College Library, Cambridge.
HEH.	Henry E. Huntington, New York.
HLE.	H. L. R. Edgar, New York.
HSP.	Historical Society of Pennsylvania, Philadelphia.
JCB.	John Carter Brown Library, Providence.
LC.	Library of Congress, Washington.
LCP.	Library Company of Philadelphia, Philadelphia.
M.	W. S. Mason, Evanston, Ill.
MHS.	Massachusetts Historical Society, Boston.
N.	Newberry Library, Chicago.
NJ.	New Jersey State Library, Trenton.
NJHS.	New Jersey Historical Society, Newark.
NYHS.	New York Historical Society, New York.
NYPL.	New York Public Library, New York.
P.	Pennsylvania State Library, Harrisburg.
W.	Wisconsin Historical Society, Madison.

TREATIES

ARTICLES
OF
PEACE

Between
The Moſt Serene and Mighty PRINCE

CHARLES II.

By the Grace of God,
King of *England*, *Scotland*, *France* and *Ireland*,
Defender of the Faith, &c.

And Several

Indian Kings and Queens, &c.

Concluded the 29th day of *May*, 1677.

Publiſhed by His Majeſties Command.

LONDON,
Printed by *John Bill*, *Chriſtopher Barker*, *Thomas Newcomb*
and *Henry Hills*, Printers to the Kings
Moſt Excellent Majeſty. 1677.

ARTICLES OF PEACE BETWEEN CHARLES II AND SEVERAL INDIAN KINGS AND QUEENS   CONCLUDED THE 29TH DAY OF MAY, 1677.

Printed at London, 1677

COLLATION. Quarto, pp. 18.
SIZE OF LETTERPRESS. 6$\frac{1}{16}$ x 3$\frac{11}{16}$.
COPIES LOCATED. N. HEH.

SYNOPSIS. The treaty consists of 21 articles, in which the Indians acknowledge subjection to the British Crown and the British guarantee them protection. They provide that no English settlement shall be made nearer than three miles of any Indian town and that the Indians shall be "secured and defended in their persons, goods and properties against all hurts and injuries of the English." They are also to be protected in their "Oystering Fishing and gathering of Tuchahoe Curtenemons Wild Oats Rushes buckoone or any thing else."

The treaty was signed by the Queen of Pamunkey, Queen of Waonoke, King of the Nancymond Indians, King of the Nottoways and Captain John West, Son of the Queen of Pamunkey, and their marks or totems are reproduced in facsimile, on p. 16.

1

Propofitions

Made by the Sachems *of the three* Maquas *Caſtles, to the* Mayor, Aldermen, *and* Commanalty *of the City of* Albany, *and Military Officers of the ſaid City, and County in the City-Hall,* February 25th. 1689/90

Peiter Schuyler Mayor, *with ten more Gentlemen, then preſent.*

Interpreted by *Arnout* & *Hille.*

The Names of the Sachims, *Sinnonguineſs* Speaker, *Rode, Sagoddiockquiſax, Oguedagoa. Toſoquatho, Odaguraſſe, Anhareuda, Jagogthera.*

PROPOSITIONS MADE BY THE SACHEMS OF THE THREE MAQUAS CASTLES TO THE MAYOR, ALDERMEN AND COMMONALTY AT ALBANY, 25TH FEBRUARY, 16 $\frac{89}{90}$

[*Colophon.*] *Boston. Printed by S. Green. Sold by Benjamin Harris at the London Coffee House, 1690.*

COLLATION. Quarto, pp. 12.
SIZE OF LETTERPRESS. $7\frac{1}{4}$ x $5\frac{3}{4}$.
COPY LOCATED. NYHS.

SYNOPSIS. At this council there were present Peter Schuyler, Mayor, "with ten more gentlemen," the representatives of the three Mohawk towns, eight of whom are named in the treaty, and two interpreters, Arnout and Hille.

The object of the council seems to have been the offering of condolences for the massacre at Schenectady and to advise as to what measures were to be taken. The Indians spoke first and after the usual condolences, stated that they had 100 young men out following the French and Canadian Indians and hoped for revenge. They reminded the Albanians that three years before they (the Mohawks) were at war with the French but that Corlaer "hindered them to proceed." But for that they would have prevented the French from sowing and reaping and they would not now have been in a position to do much mischief.

To the report of the council is appended an examination of three French prisoners who give an account of the force at Schenectady with some details of the fight as well as much information as to the state of Canada and some preparations that were being made to attack Albany.

This Treaty was reprinted in the NYHS. Collections for 1869, pp. 165 *et seq.*

2

THE
ANSWER
OF
The Five Nations,
VIZ.

The *Mahaques, Oneydes, Onnondages, Cajouges* and *Senekes,*

TO THE
QUESTION
Put to Them in *May* laft
By His Excellency

Benjamin Fletcher, Captain General and Governour in Chief of the Province of *New-York*, Province of *Pennfilvania*, Country of *New-Caftle*, and the Territories and Tracts of Land depending thereon in *America*, and Vice-Admiral of the fame; Their Majefties Lieutenant and Commander in Chief of the Militia, and of the Forces by Sea and Land within Their Majefties Collony of *Connecticut*, and of all the Forts and Places of Strength within the fame.

Given at *Albany* the 15th day of *Auguft*, 1694.

Prefcat

ACCOUNT OF A TREATY BETWEEN GOVERNOR FLETCHER AND THE FIVE NATIONS, AUGUST, 1694.

[New York, Wm. Bradford, 1694.]

COLLATION. Pp. 39, A-K in twos. The first two leaves have no pagination. The third leaf begins 5. The verso of last leaf blank. Sigs. A and I not marked.

SIZE OF LEAF. 7¾ x 5¾.

COPY LOCATED. BM.

SYNOPSIS. On verso of title "Lisenced, David Jamison." P. 3: Heading filling whole page as reproduced. Proceedings pp. [4] to top half of p. 10; continuing on lower half of same page. "At a meeting at Albany the 16th Day of August, 1694" to p. 15; continuing, "At a meeting at Albany the 17th Day of August, 1694" to p. 18; continuing, "A conference held at a private House in Albany the 20th of August, 1694" to p. 28; continuing, "At a meeting at Albany the 22th Day of August, 1694" to p. 31. Pp. 32–33: The Address of the River Indians to his Excellency Benjamin Fletcher, etc., at Albany, August 18th, 1694. Pp. 34–35: The Answer which his Excellency Benjamin Fletcher, etc., gave to the River Indians, August 22nd, 1694. Pp. 36–39: "A Conference had between his Excellency Benjamin Fletcher, etc., and the *Mahikanders* or Lower River Indians and *Showannos* or Far Indians, at *Kingstone* in the County of *Ulster* the 28th of August, 1694." Ends FINIS on p. 39.

[I can learn of only one copy of this book which is in the British Museum. I am indebted to the kindness of Mr. Henry N. Stevens for the reproductions and description here given.—H. F. DEP.]

An account of this treaty is printed in the NYHS. Coll., 1869, pp. 409–415.

A
JOURNAL

Of what Passed in the Expedition of

His Excellency

Coll. *Benjunin Fletcher*, Captain General and Governour in Chief of the Province of *New-York*, *&c.* To *ALBANY*, to Renew the Covenant Chain with the five Canton Nations of *Indians*, the *Mohaques*, *Oneydes*, *Onondages*, *Cajouges* and *Sinnekes*.

September 17. 1696. ON *Thursday* after Sun set his Excellency imbarqued at *Greenwich*. On *Tuesday* morning arrived at *Albany*.

This day his Excellency viewed the Fortifications of the City, and gave orders to the Mayor & Aldermen for such Reparations as were found needful in the Block-houses, Platforms and Stockadoes.

The 27th, *Sunday* afternoon, The Sachims of *Oneid* and *Onondage* arrived at *Albany*, in the Evening they supped with his Excellency giving great expressions of the Joy and Satisfaction they had in meeting his Excellency.

The 28th, his Excellency sent Capt. *James Weems* to view the Garrison at *Schenectady*, and bring report to his Excellency what necessary Repairs are wanting. Which was performed accordingly.

This

JOURNAL OF WHAT PASSED, ETC., BE-
TWEEN GOVERNOR FLETCHER AND
THE FIVE NATIONS AT ALBANY, SEP-
TEMBER, 1696.

[*New York, Wm. Bradford, 1696*].

COLLATION. Quarto, pp. 11.
SIZE OF LEAF. 5⅜ x 7.
COPY LOCATED. BM.

SYNOPSIS. P. I—Title, caption, etc., as reproduced.

Pp. 2–3—At a meeting of the Sachems of the Five Nations at
Albany the 29th of Sept., 1696.

Pp. 4–5—Ditto, 1st October, 1696.

Pp. 6–7—Ditto, 2d October, 1696.

Pp. 8–11—At a private meeting of the Sachems at Albany the
3rd of October, 1696.

The only copy located is in the British Museum. The reproduction and
above description furnished by Mr. Henry N. Stevens.

4

Propositions made by the Five Nations of Indians, viz. The *Mohaques, Oneydes, Onnondages, Cayouges & Sinnekes,* to his Excellency Richard Earl of *Bellomont,* Capt General and Governour in chief his Majesties Province of *New-York, &c.* in *Albany,* the 20th of *July, Anno Dom.* 1698

PRESENT

His Excellency *Richard* Earl of *Bellomont,* Captain General & Governour in Chief of *New-York, &c.*

Capt. *Johannes Schuyler,*
Hendrick van Rensselaer,
Jan Lansingh,
Jan Vinnagen, } Aldermen.
Hendrick Hanse,
Wessell ten Brock,

Capt. *Johannes Bleeker,* } Assistants,
Johannes Themese,

And several other Gentlemen.

Coll. *Peter Schuyler,*
James Graham, Esq; Attorney General
Coll. *Abraham D' Peyster.*
Walter Hungerford, Esq;
Major *Derick Wessells,* Mayor,
Capt. *John Janse Bleeker,* Recorder.

PROPOSITIONS MADE TO GOVERNOR BELLOMONT BY THE FIVE NATIONS IN JULY, 1698, AT ALBANY.

Printed at New York by Wm. Bradford

COLLATION. Folio, pp. 22.
SIZE OF LETTERPRESS. 9½ x 5⅜.
COPY LOCATED. NYHS.

SYNOPSIS. There were present Governor Bellomont and a numerous retinue and the representatives of all of the Five Nations; the Interpreters were Cornelius Velie and Helletie van Olanda. The conference convened on July 20. Governor Bellomont was suffering with gout. The Indians complained of an alleged sale of land by a few of the Mohawks and claimed that it was illegal and asked to have the "Writing" burned. They complained also of the attacks of the French and their Indian allies after peace was declared and of the high price of goods. They state further "that a greater evil could not have attended all of us in the five Nations as well as the brethren than the suffering the French to re-settle Candarque which will always be as a thorn in our sides and keep us in such a continual alarm and watchfulness that we shall never be able to hunt freely whilst such a power and fortress is so near not only to annoy but in a capacity to destroy us." In the discussion on this matter the Indians took occasion to correct the Governor by reciting the whole history of the negotiations and acts of Governor Fletcher relating to Candarque.

The conferences lasted until July 27th and a complete daily report is given of them. Besides these reports the printed account gives an Examination of Skachkook Indians in reference to murders at Hatfield; The Governor's report of the Albany meeting to the Council; Instructions to Col. Peter Schuyler; A Message sent by the Five Nations in August regarding their friends who were captives in Canada.

See Winsor Nar. and Crit. Hist., V, 483, 560.

George Town

On *Arrowsick* Island Aug. 9th. 1717.

Annoque Regni Regis GEORGII *Magnæ Britanniæ,*&c.Quarto.

A Conference of His Excellency the GOVERNOUR, with the 𝕾𝖆𝖈𝖍𝖊𝖒𝖘 and Chief Men of the Eastern 𝕴𝖓𝖉𝖎𝖆𝖓𝖘.

GEORGETOWN ON ARROWSICK ISLAND 9TH AUGUST, 1717. A CONFERENCE OF THE GOVERNOR WITH THE SACHEMS OF THE EASTERN INDIANS.

[Colophon:] Boston. B. Green, 1717

COLLATION. Pp. 13. No title page. Caption title.
LETTERPRESS. 6⅝ x 4⅝.
COPIES LOCATED. AAS. JCB. LC. HLE.

SYNOPSIS. The Governor opened the congress by a speech in which he refers to various previous treaties with the Indians.

The Indians object to the construction of a Fort but are told by the Governor that he will build a fort where he pleases. He claims land on the Kennebec River to which the Indians demur. Finally the conference is ended by the Indians withdrawing "in a hasty, abrupt manner without taking leave, and left behind them their English Colours." Later they brought to the Governor a letter of Sebastion Rasles, the Jesuit missionary, containing a message of Vaudreuill to the Indians in reference to their lands and promising help.

This Treaty is in the Maine Hist. Soc. Coll., iii, 361, and in N. H. Prov. Papers, iii, 693. See Winsor Nar. and Crit. Hist., V, 424, for other references.

The PARTICULARS of an

INDIAN TREATY
At CONESTOGOE,
BETWEEN

His Excellency Sir *William Keith*, Bart. Governor of *Pennsylvania,*
And the Deputies of the Five Nations.

Publifhed at the Requeft of the GENTLEMEN who were prefent,
and waited upon the Governor in His Journey.

THE PARTICULARS OF AN INDIAN TREATY AT CONESTOGOE BETWEEN HIS EXCELLENCY SIR WILLIAM KEITH, BART., GOVERNOR OF PENNSYLVANIA, AND THE DEPUTIES OF THE FIVE NATIONS, IN JULY, 1721.

Printed by Andrew Bradford at Philadelphia

COLLATION. Small folio, pp. 8. Sigs. A and B. Caption title.
LETTERPRESS. 10¼ x 5⅝.
COPIES LOCATED. D. HEH.

SYNOPSIS.

July 5. Complimentary speeches.

July 6. Governor Keith tells the Conestoga Indians that he has arranged with the Governor of Virginia to make the Potomac the boundary of the hunting territory between them and the Virginia Indians.

July 7. Ghesaont, a Seneca, presents a belt of wampum and seven bundles of skins and makes a friendly speech in which he complains of the sale of liquor to the Indians and the small price paid for furs.

THE
PARTICULARS
OF AN
Indian Treaty
AT
CONESTOGOE,

BETWEEN

His Excellency Sir WILLIAM KEITH,
Bart. Governor of *Pennsylvania,* and
the Deputies of the Five Nations.

Publiſhed

At the Requeſt of the GENTLEMEN
who were preſent, and waited upon
the Governor in His Journey.

DUBLIN

Re-Printed, by *Elizabeth Sadleir,* for
Samuel Fuller, at the *Globe* and *Scales,*
in *Meath Street,* MDCCXXIII.

July 8. Governor Keith makes a speech of friendship with the usual presents and warns the Five Nations that they cannot pass through the colony to make war on Indians friendly to the government of Virginia. He counsels them to peace with the English and other Indians but warns them that the French are artful and not to be trusted. He promises that wrongs done them by white men will be avenged and that he will see that they are fairly treated by the traders. He says he would like to stop the liquor traffic but the Indians make that impossible.

Present at the Treaty: Governor Keith, Richard Hill, Caleb Pusey, Jonathan Dickinson, Col. John French, James Logan, Secretary, "with divers gentlemen," Deputies from the Senecas, Onondagas, and Cayugas; Interpreters Smith the Ganewese-Indian, John Cartledge, and James le Tort.

7

TREATY AT CONESTOGOE IN JULY, 1721

Reprinted at Dublin, 1723

COLLATION. Small octavo, pp. 48.
SIZE OF LETTERPRESS. 5½ x 2⅞.
COPY LOCATED. LCP.

SYNOPSIS. This is a volume containing the Treaty of July 5–8 at Conestogoe, pp. 1 to 27, Treaty at Albany, September, 1722, pp. 28–45, and the Dying Words of Ocanickon, pp. 46–48.

Mr. Hildeburn in "Issues of the Press of Pennsylvania," No. 172, says this Treaty was reprinted at Dublin and London in 1723 but I have not found a copy of the London edition.

8

A
TREATY
OF
Peace and Friendſhip

Made and Concluded between His Excellency

Sir WILLIAM KEITH, Bart,

Governor of the Province of

Pennſylvania

For and on Behalf of the ſaid Province

AND THE

Chiefs of the *Indians* of the Five Nations.

At *ALBANY*, in the Month of *September*, 1722.

TREATY BETWEEN GOVERNOR KEITH OF PENNSYLVANIA AND THE FIVE NATIONS MADE AT ALBANY IN SEPTEMBER, 1722.

Printed at Dublin, 1723

COLLATION. This Treaty occupies pp. 28 to 45 of a volume containing the Treaty of 1721, Conestogoe [which see], and the Dying Words of Ocanickon. COPY LOCATED. LCP.

SYNOPSIS. New York, Pennsylvania and Virginia were represented at this council by their Governors, who sailed up the Hudson on a sloop leaving New York August 17th, and arriving at Albany August 20th. This volume contains only so much of the council minutes as relates to Pennsylvania. It consists nominally of the affair of an Indian killed by white traders near Conestogoe but the speeches of Governor Keith were very conciliatory and the "chain of friendship brightened."

9

THE PARTICULARS OF AN INDIAN TREATY AT CONESTOGOE BETWEEN HIS EXCELLENCY SIR WILLIAM KEITH, BART., GOVERNOR OF PENNSYLVANIA, AND THE DEPUTIES OF THE FIVE NATIONS IN JUNE, 1722.

Philadelphia, Andrew Bradford, 1722

The above title is taken from Hildeburn's "Issues of the Press of Pennsylvania," No. 186. No copy is located by him and it is evident that he had never seen one. Possibly he took the title from an advertisement in a contemporary newspaper.

10

THE

CONFERENCE

With the Eastern Indians, at the Ratification
of the PEACE, held at *Falmouth* in *Casco-Bay*,
in *July* and *August*, 1 7 2 6.

CONFERENCE WITH THE EASTERN IN-DIANS AT FALMOUTH IN CASCO BAY IN JULY AND AUGUST, 1726.

[*Colophon:*] *"Boston: Printed for Benj. Eliot, at his shop in King Street where may also be had the former Printed Conference with the Eastern Indians."*

COLLATION. Pp. 23, A-F in twos.
SIZE OF LETTERPRESS. 7⅝ x 5¼.
COPIES LOCATED. AAS. LC. MHS.

SYNOPSIS. The conference lasted from 16th July to August 11th. About forty Penobscots only were present. The English were much annoyed to find no other tribes there to ratify a peace made at Boston the previous winter. The Indians added to this annoyance by a suggestion that a conference should be held at Mont. Royal (Montreal). They were told that it was beneath English dignity to treat with Indians on French soil.

The Indians demanded the removal of two houses at Richmond and St. George, with which the English refused to comply. The Indians claimed that they did not possess a single English captive.

This Treaty and the one in Falmouth, 1727, were reprinted in Boston, 1754, by S. Kneeland, 4to, pp. 20, 27.

There is a copy of this reprint at AAS. See Winsor Nar. and Crit. Hist., V, 432, for other references to this Treaty.

11

THE
CONFERENCE

With the Eaſtern Indians at the furthei
Ratification of the PEACE, Held at *Falmouth* in *Caſco-Bay*, in *July* 1727.

Falmouth, July 11th. 1727.

CONFERENCE WITH THE EASTERN IN-
DIANS AT THE FURTHER RATIFICA-
TION OF THE PEACE, HELD AT FAL-
MOUTH IN CASCO BAY, IN JULY, 1727.

Printed at Boston 1727

COLLATION. Quarto, pp. 31. A–H in twos. Caption title. No colophon.
LETTERPRESS. 7¼ x 5¼.
COPY LOCATED. AAS.

SYNOPSIS. The selection of Falmouth as a meeting place seems
to have been objectionable to the Indians who with the exception of
the Penobscots refused to go there the year before. This year the
same objection was made but a ship was sent for them and the
Norridgewocks and Wowenocks came. The treaty, dated Boston,
15th December, 1725, was read and confirmed by the signatures of
the four chiefs whose totems are reproduced. It attempts to settle
the disputes as to land, captives, etc.

This Treaty was reprinted in 1754 with the Treaty of 1726. See Winsor
Nar. and Crit. Hist., V, 432.

CONFERENCE BETWEEN GOVERNOR BELCHER AND INDIANS OF THE PENOBSCOTS, NORRIDGEWOCKS, PIGWACKETS, AND AINERSCOGGINS AT FALMOUTH AND CASCO BAY, JULY, 1732.

Printed at Boston by B. Green

COLLATION. Quarto pp. 23 with a slip of Errata pasted on p. [24]. Sigs. A—F in twos.

SIZE OF LETTERPRESS. 7⅛ x 4¹¹⁄₁₆.

COPIES LOCATED AAS. D. N. JCB. LC.

SYNOPSIS. One cannot read this treaty and not be struck with the difference between the methods used with these Eastern Indians and the method followed by New York, Pennsylvania and Virginia with the Six Nations and kindred tribes. All these latter conferences and treaties were marked by great dignity and the following of set forms. No speech ever went unanswered and it was seldom answered the same day but only after taking time for deliberation. At Falmouth, Governor Belcher replied to the Indian speeches at once and pressed the Indians for immediate answers. They told him they did things only after deliberating among themselves, but it made no difference to the Governor, nor did he mark his answers with presents as the Indians did.

The Governor had been to inspect the English forts at St. George's, Brunswick, Richmond, etc., and had invited these Indians to meet him. His principal business with them seemed to be to advise them to give up the French religion and adopt that of the English and to drink less rum. The Indians tried to transact other business such as arranging for proper trading posts, regulation of hunting rights, etc., but they got short answers from His Excellency.

This Treaty was reprinted at London, 1732, and there are copies of the reprint at JCB. and Harvard. See Winsor Nar. and Crit. Hist., V, 432.

14

A

CONFERENCE

of His Excellency

Jonathan Belcher, Esq;

Captain General and Governour in Chief of His Majesty's
Province of the 𝕸𝖆𝖘𝖘𝖆𝖈𝖍𝖚𝖘𝖊𝖙𝖙𝖘-𝕭𝖆𝖞 in 𝕹𝖊𝖜-
𝕰𝖓𝖌𝖑𝖆𝖓𝖉, with 𝕰𝖉𝖊𝖜𝖆𝖐𝖊𝖓𝖐 Chief Sachem of the
𝕻𝖊𝖓𝖔𝖇𝖘𝖈𝖚𝖙 Tribe, 𝕷𝖔𝖗𝖔𝖓 one of the Chief Captains
of the same Tribe, 𝕷𝖔𝖗𝖚𝖘 Chief Sachem of the
𝕸𝖔𝖗𝖗𝖎𝖉𝖌𝖊𝖜𝖔𝖈𝖐 Tribe, 𝕬𝖉𝖎𝖆𝖜𝖆𝖓𝖉𝖔 Chief Sachem
of the 𝕻𝖎𝖌𝖜𝖆𝖈𝖐𝖊𝖙 Tribe, and 𝕸𝖊𝖉𝖆𝖌𝖆𝖓𝖊𝖘𝖘𝖊𝖙 Chief
Sachem of the 𝕬𝖒𝖊𝖗𝖊𝖘𝖈𝖔𝖌𝖌𝖎𝖓 Tribe, with other
Chief Men of the said 𝕴𝖓𝖉𝖎𝖆𝖓 Tribes at 𝕱𝖆𝖑𝖒𝖔𝖚𝖙𝖍
in 𝕮𝖆𝖘𝖈𝖔-𝕭𝖆𝖞, 𝕵𝖚𝖑𝖞 1732. Annoq; Regni Regis
GEORGIJ; Secundi, Magnæ Britanniæ, &c. Sexto.
Falmouth, Monday, *July* 24. 1732.

FACSIMILE TITLE OF No. 14

TWO

INDIAN TREATIES

THE ONE HELD AT

CONESTOGOE

In *MAY* 1728.

AND THE OTHER AT

PHILADELPHIA

In *JUNE* following,

BETWEEN

The Honourable *PATRICK GORDON* Efq; Lieut. Governour of the Province of *Pennfylvania,* and Counties of *New-Caftle, Kent,* and *Suffex* upon *Delaware,*

AND

The Chiefs of the *Coneftogoe, Delaware, Shawanefe* and *Canawefe Indians.*

TAKEN from the Minutes of Council, and publifhed by Authority.

THe *Governour having laft Fall acquainted the* Indians *of* Coneftogoe, *by Mr* Wright, *that he defigned to vifit them, fo foon as their People were come home ont of the Woods in the Spring, received an Account about three Weeks fince from Mr* Wright, *that Capt.* Civility *the Chief of thofe Indians with his People were returned : Whereupon the Governour difpatched an Exprefs to acquaint the Indians, that he would meet them about the* 23d *of May Inftant at* Coneftogoe, *where he defired that the Chiefs, of all the Indians might be prefent, and that Capt* Civility *would difpatch Meffengers to* Saffoonan, Opekaffet *and* Manawky- hickon *Chiefs of the* Delawares, *who live up the River* Safquehannah *to be there.*

Purfuant to this Appointment, the Governour attended with fome Members of Council, and divers other Gentlemen, to the Number of about Thirty, *who voluntarily offered their Company thither, fet out from* Philadelphia *on the* 22d *of May, and on the 22d in the Evening came to the Houfe of Mr.* Andrew Cornifh, *about a Mile diftant from the* Indian-Town. *The* 24. *and* 25th *Days were fpent in waiting for fome other Perfons expected at the Treaty, and in mutual Civilities, and on the* 26th *the Treaty began as follows.*

TWO INDIAN TREATIES HELD AT CONESTOGOE IN MAY, 1728, AND AT PHILADELPHIA, IN JUNE, 1728.

[Colophon:] Printed by Andrew Bradford, Phila.

COLLATION. Folio, pp. 17. Sigs. [A] to D in twos.
SIZE OF LETTERPRESS. 10 x 5½.
COPY LOCATED. LCP.

SYNOPSIS. The meeting at Conestogoe was May 26th and 27th. Attended by Lt.-Gov. Gordon and others and Indians of the Conestoga, Delaware, Shawanese, and Canawese tribes. The Governor related the details of trouble between the whites and Indians at Mahanatawny Iron Works and at the house of John Burt.

The meeting at Philadelphia was June 4th and 5th. Deeds of lands from the Indians dated September, 1718, were shown to the Indians to assure them that said lands had been paid for and this deed is printed in the treaty as is also the petition of Palatines in regard to their land.

13

A

CONFERENCE

Between his Excellency

Jonathan Belcher Esq;

Captain-General and Governour in Chief

Of His MAJESTY's Province

O F

Maſſachuſet's-Bay in *New-England:*

AND THE

CHIEF SACHEMS

O F

Several INDIAN TRIBES, with other CHIEF MEN of the ſaid Tribes,

At FALMOUTH. in CASCO-BAY, in *New-England,* *July* 1732. Annoq; Regni Regis GEORGII Secundi, Magnæ Britanniæ, &c. Sexto.

LONDON.

Printed for N. CHOLMONDELEY, at the Corner of *Thavies-Inn, Holbourn;* and ſold by E. NUTT, at the *Royal-Exchange;* A. DODD, without *Temple-Bar;* and the Bookſellers of *London* and *Weſtminſter.*

(*Price Sixpence.*)

AT A
CONFERENCE

Held at *Deèrfield* in the County of *Hampſhire*, the Twenty ſeventh Day of *Auguſt*, Anno Regni Regis GEORGIJ Secundi, Magnæ, Britanniæ, Franciæ et Hiberniæ, &c. Nono, *Annoq;* *Domini*, 1735. By & between His Excellency

JONATHAN BELCHER, Eſq;

Captain General and Governour in Chief in and over His Majeſty's Province of the *Maſſachuſetts-Bay* in *New England*.

AND

Duntauſſoogoe and others, Chiefs of the *Cagnawaga* Tribe of Indians, &c. who were accompanied by a Number of the *St. Francois* Indians, who at their own deſire were included in the Treaty with the *Cagnawagas*, the whole being Twentyſeven.

Cuncaupot Captain, with his Lieutenant and ſeveral others of the Chiefs of the *Houſſatonuoc* Indians &c. being upwards of Forty in the whole.

Marſequunt, Naunautooghijau, and **Weenpauk,** Three Chiefs of the *Scautacook* Tribe and others, including Seventeen of the *Moheegs*, making Eighty in the whole.

A   His

CONFERENCE AT DEERFIELD, 27TH AUGUST, 1735, BETWEEN GOVERNOR BELCHER AND THE CAUGHNAWAGAS, ST. FRANCIS, HOUSSTONNOUCS, SCHATIGCOKES AND MOHEGAN TRIBES.

[Boston, 1735]

COLLATION. Pp. 19, A–F in twos.
LETTERPRESS. 7¾ x 5¼.
COPIES LOCATED. AAS. BPL. JCB. LC.

SYNOPSIS. About 140 Indians were present. Unlike the conferences with the Eastern Indians much formality was observed and wampum belts exchanged. Peace was renewed. The Indians were well entertained but no business of importance was transacted. During the conference Rev. John Sargeant was ordained in the presence of the Governor and the Indians.

This was reprinted in Maine Hist. Coll., IV, 123. See Winsor Nar. and Crit. Hist., V, 433.

A TREATY

OF

FRIENDSHIP

HELD WITH THE

CHIEFS OF THE SIX NATIONS,

AT

PHILADELPHIA,

IN

SEPTEMBER and *OCTOBER*, 1736.

PHILADELPHIA:
Printed and Sold by B. FRANKLIN, at the New Printing-Office
near the Market. M,DCC,XXXVII.

TREATY HELD AT PHILADELPHIA BEGIN-NING SEPTEMBER 28, 1736, WITH THE SIX NATIONS.

Printed by Franklin at Philadelphia, 1737

COLLATION. Folio, pp. 14. Sigs. [A] to D in twos.
SIZE OF LETTERPRESS. 10 x 5½.
COPIES LOCATED. HSP. CPC.

SYNOPSIS. Except the Mohawks, all the Six Nations were represented. There were about 100 Indians in all. Thomas Penn and James Logan were present, with Conrad Weiser as interpreter. The preliminary council was held at James Logan's at Stenton. They were informed that while the council would be held at Philadelphia that as there was smallpox in the town they should not spend much time there.

The object of the treaty was to confirm the one made four years before.

16

THE
TREATY

HELD WITH THE

INDIANS

OF THE

SIX NATIONS,

AT

PHILADELPHIA,

In *JULY*, 1742.

PHILADELPHIA:

Printed and Sold by B. F R A N K L I N, at the New-Printing-Office, near the Market. M,DCC,XLIII.

TREATY WITH THE SIX NATIONS AT PHILADELPHIA, JULY 2–12, 1742.

Printed by Franklin at Philadelphia, 1743

COLLATION. Folio, pp. 25. Sigs. [A] to F in twos, with the leaf forming p. 25.

SIZE OF LETTERPRESS. 10½ x 5½.

COPIES LOCATED. D. APS. CPC. HLE. NYPL.

SYNOPSIS. There were present at this treaty delegates from the Onondagas, Cayugas, Oneidas, Senecas, Tuscaroras, Shawanese, Nanticokes, and Delawares; and one entire page is filled with the names of these delegates. The council was presided over by George Thomas, lieutenant-governor, with Conrad Weiser and Cornelius Spring as interpreters. The presents made to the Indians are specified.

The principal business was to settle the complaints that each side made against the other of encroachments on their lands. The whites promised to remove their people from the Indian lands and the Indians gave a like promise. One of the claims made by the whites was that fifty years before they had bought land at the Forks of the Delaware from the Delawares which the latter now refused to vacate. After the Indians had investigated this claim Canassatego made his famous speech to the Delawares. "But how came you to take upon you to sell land at all? We conquered you; we made women of you; you know that you are women and can no more sell land than women; nor is it fit that you should have the power to sell land since you abuse it. This land that you claim is gone through your guts. You have been furnished with clothes, meat and drink by the goods paid you for it; and now you want it again like children as you are," etc.

17

THE
TREATY

Held with the

INDIANS

OF THE

SIX NATIONS

AT

Philadelphia, in *July* 1742.

To which is Prefix'd

An Account of the *first Confederacy* of the *SIX NATIONS*, their present TRIBUTARIES, DEPENDENTS, and ALLIES.

LONDON:

Re-printed and Sold by T. SOWLE RAYLTON and LUKE HINDE, at the *Bible* George-Yard, Lombard-Street.

[Price Six-Pence.]

It was also at this treaty that the Indians expressed their good opinions of James Logan and Conrad Weiser. Of the latter they said: "The Business the Five Nations transact with you is of great consequence and requires a skillful and honest person to go between us, one in whom both you and we can place Confidence. We esteem our present Interpreter to be such a person, equally faithful in the interpretation of whatever is said to him by either of us; equally allied to both; he is of our nation and a member of our Council as well as yours. When we adopted him we divided him into two equal parts. One we kept for ourselves and one we left for you. He has had a great deal of trouble for us, wore out his shoes in our messages and dirtied his clothes by being amongst us so that he has become as nasty as an Indian."

This Treaty was reprinted in Colden's " History of the Five Indian Nations of Canada," London, 1747, p. 45.

18

THE TREATY WITH THE SIX NATIONS. REPRINT OF TREATY AT PHILADELPHIA, 1742.

London [n. d. 1747 ?]

COLLATION.   Octavo, pp. xii, 37 [1].
SIZE OF LETTERPRESS.   6¾ x 3¾.
COPIES LOCATED.   D. HSP. N. W. JCB. M. HC.

SYNOPSIS.   The preface to this edition has a list of twenty Indian tribes with their numbers, place of residence and their relations with the English and Six Nations.   It refers to Colden's "History of the Five Nations," which, it says, is ready for the press and soon to be printed, referring, of course, to the first London edition of that book, 1747.

19

A
CONFERENCE

Held at the Fort at *St. George*'s in the County of *York*, the fourth Day of *August*, *Anno Regm Regis* GEORGIJ *Secundi*, Magnæ Britanniæ, Franciæ *et* Hiberniæ,*&c. Decimo Sexto*, Annoq; Domini, 1 7 4 2.

BETWEEN

His Excellency

WILLIAM SHIRLEY, Esq;

Captain General and Governour in Chief in and over His Majesty's Province of the *Massachusetts-Bay* in *New-England*.

AND THE

Chief Sachems & Captains

OF THE

Penobscott, Norridgewock, Pigwaket or Amiscogging or Saco, St. John's, Bescommonconty or Amerescogging and St. Francis Tribes of *INDIANS*.

August 2. 1 7 4 2.

CONFERENCE AT ST. GEORGE'S THE 4TH DAY OF AUGUST, 1742, BETWEEN WILLIAM SHIRLEY AND THE CHIEF SACHEMS AND CAPTAINS OF THE PENOBSCOT NORRIDGEWOCKS, ETC.

[*Colophon:*] *Boston: Printed by J. Draper, 1742*

COLLATION. Quarto, pp. 19. A–E in twos.
LETTERPRESS. 7¾ x 5½.
COPIES LOCATED. AAS. JCB. HEH. LC. MHS.

SYNOPSIS. The Council began on the 2nd of August and closed on the 7th. On his arrival in Boston, Governor Shirley had sent a letter to those tribes notifying them of his appointment as Governor and notifying them that if they wished to send delegates to him they would be transported in the Province sloop. Accordingly they sent two delegates to Boston in December who laid before the Governor their difficulties in trade "arising from a scarcity of provisions, tobacco, powder and shot, and the truck master not understanding your language, and desired that two men might be appointed twice a year to view the truck houses; and that an account of the prices of beaver peltry and other goods might be publicly posted there." The Governor had promised to examine their complaints and the greater part of this conference was occupied in settling them.

See Winsor Nar. and Crit. Hist., V, 434.

20

GOVERNOR AND COMPANY OF CONNECTICUT,

AND

MOHEAGAN INDIANS, BY THEIR GUARDIANS.

CERTIFIED COPY

OF

BOOK OF PROCEEDINGS

BEFORE

COMMISSIONERS OF REVIEW,

MDCCXLIII.

LONDON
PRINTED BY W. AND J. RICHARDSON.
MDCCLXIX.

GOVERNOR AND COMPANY OF CONNECTICUT AND MOHEGAN INDIANS, 1743.

Printed at London in 1769

COLLATION. Quarto, pp. [2], xxi, 283. Folding map.
SIZE OF LETTERPRESS. 8⅝ x 5½.
COPIES SEEN. NYHS.

SYNOPSIS. While this work is not the record of a treaty or Indian council, but rather a report of the evidence taken in the trial to determine the rights of the Mohegan Indians to land claimed by them and the Colony of Connecticut, it is included here on account of its relating to Indian lands about which so many treaties were made. The great length of the work prevents any adequate synopsis. The commissioners appointed to consider the cause were the Governors of New York and New Jersey with their respective councils or any five or more of them. The five who tried the cause were Cadwalader Colden, Phillip Cortlandt, and Daniel Horsmanden, of New York; and John Rodman and Robt. Hunter Morris, of New Jersey. The evidence submitted consisted of public records, Indian deeds, etc., which are copied in this report, as is also Mason's Pequot War which was put in evidence. The great importance of this record cannot be adequately shown in a brief notice. To the decision rendered Messrs. Horsmanden and Morris dissented and Mr. Horsmanden's opinion in dissent was printed in London, 1769.

21

A

TREATY,

Held at the Town of

Lancaster, in PENNSYLVANIA,

By the HONOURABLE the

Lieutenant-Governor of the PROVINCE,

And the HONOURABLE the

Commissioners for the PROVINCES

OF

VIRGINIA *and* MARYLAND,

WITH THE

I N D I A N S

OF THE

SIX NATIONS,

In *JUNE*, 1744.

PHILADELPHIA:

Printed and Sold by B. FRANKLIN, at the New-Printing-Office, near the Market. M,DCC,XLIV.

TREATY HELD AT LANCASTER, PA., WITH THE SIX NATIONS, IN JUNE, 1744.

Printed at Philadelphia by Franklin in 1744

COLLATION. Folio, pp. 39. Sigs. A to K in twos.
SIZE OF LETTERPRESS. 10¼ x 5½.
COPIES LOCATED. D. NYHS. LCP. HSP. NYPL. Friend. APS. CPC. N. BPL. W. JCB. M. HEH. HLE.

SYNOPSIS. The council was convened on Friday, June 22, 1744, Lt.-Gov. George Thomas of Pennsylvania presiding, with deputies from Maryland and Virginia and from the Senecas, Onondagas, Oneidas, Cayugas, and Tuscaroras, with Conrad Weiser as Interpreter.

This treaty was held to settle the disputes between the colonies of Maryland and Virginia and the Six Nations relative to lands claimed by the Indians in those colonies. It was of such importance that it lasted until July 4th and produced a great deal of discussion in which the Indians showed much ability and a knowledge of the history of Indian affairs. The troubles were finally adjusted and payment was made to the Indians. It was during the meetings of this treaty that the Governor of Maryland received the name Tocarryhogan.

The troubles between the Six Nations and the Cherokees and Catawbas were mentioned and the Indians gave the Council a statement of the trouble.

The death of John Armstrong, an Indian trader, was discussed and the Indians promised satisfaction for his murder.

Franklin mentions this Treaty in a letter to Wm. Strahan dated Sept. 18, 1744, and says he is sending Strahan 200 copies for sale. This statement probably indicates that a large number of copies were printed, which may account for its apparently being less rare than most of the other issues.

22

THE
TREATY
Held with the
INDIANS
OF THE
SIX NATIONS,
AT

Lancaster, in *Pennsylvania*, in
June, 1744.

To which is prefix'd,

An Account of the *first Confederacy* of the SIX
NATIONS, their present TRIBUTARIES, DE-
PENDENTS, and ALLIES, and of their RELIGION,
and Form of GOVERNMENT.

WILLIAMSBURG:
Printed and Sold by WILLIAM PARKS.

TREATY AT LANCASTER IN JUNE, 1744.

Reprinted at Williamsburg, Va., by William Parks

COLLATION. Octavo, pp. xii + 79.

SIZE OF LETTERPRESS. 7 x 3⅞.

COPIES LOCATED. NYHS. HC. N. JCB.

This Treaty was also reprinted in Colden's "History of the Five Indian Nations of Canada," London, 1747, p. 87.

There is a Journal of Witham Marshe, secretary of the Maryland Commissioners, kept during this treaty published by the Mass. Hist. Soc., Coll. vii, 171. It was also reprinted at Lancaster, 1884, with annotations by W. H. Egle with the following title:

Lancaster in 1744 | Journal | of the | Treaty at Lancaster | In 1744 | with the Six Nations | By Witham Marshe, | Secretary of the Maryland Commissioners | Annotated by William H. Egle, M.D. | Lancaster, Pa. | The New Era Steam Book and Job Print. | 1884. | 4to pp. 30.

See also Winsor Nar. and Crit. Hist., V, 566.

23

AN
ACCOUNT
OF THE
TREATY

Held at the CITY of

Albany, in the Province of *NEW-YORK*,

By His EXCELLENCY the

Governor of that PROVINCE,

And the HONOURABLE the

COMMISSIONERS for the Provinces

OF

MASSACHUSETTS, CONNECTICUT,

AND

PENNSYLVANIA,

WITH THE

INDIANS
OF THE
SIX NATIONS,

In *OCTOBER*, 1745.

PHILADELPHIA:
Printed by B. FRANKLIN, at the NEW-PRINTING-OFFICE,
near the Market, M,DCC,XLVI.

TREATY HELD AT ALBANY IN OCTOBER, 1745, BETWEEN THE PROVINCES OF MASSACHUSETTS, CONNECTICUT, AND PENNSYLVANIA AND THE SIX NATIONS.

Printed by Franklin at Philadelphia, 1746

COLLATION. Folio, pp. 20.
SIZE OF LETTERPRESS. 9⅝ x 5½.
COPIES LOCATED. D. LCP. NYPL. Friend. CPC. M.

SYNOPSIS. There were present at this treaty the Governor and deputies of New York and Commissioners from the Colonies of Massachusetts, Connecticut, and Pennsylvania, and Indians from all of the Six Nations except the Senecas. At a preliminary meeting of the Commissioners it was resolved that the New York and New England delegates should make a joint speech to the Indians and that afterward the Pennsylvania Commissioners should hold a separate council.

The joint speech of New York and New England told the Indians of the war that then existed between France and Great Britain, of the attacks and depredations of the French and their Indian allies against the English settlements, and advised the Six Nations to join the Colonies in retaliation. It reproved the Mohawks for treating with the French at Montreal a few months before. The Indians replied that they were true friends of the English and would not permit the French or their Indian Allies to cross their lands to attack the English, but that before they declared war it was necessary that they should first demand satisfaction of the Canadian Indians which would require about two months' time. They explained their conference with the French at Montreal. The answer was satisfactory to all except the Massachusetts commissioners who said that the year before at a conference at Boston between the Mohawks and Eastern Indians the former had reproved the latter for hostility to the English and threatened them with war if they committed any hostile acts. In this connection there is an interesting reference to the Boston conference in the "Itinerarium of Dr. Alexander Hamilton," privately printed by Mr. W. K. Bixby, St. Louis, 1907. Hamilton was in Boston in July, 1744, and records in his diary of July 24th, some ac-

A TREATY,

BETWEEN

HIS EXCELLENCY

The Honourable GEORGE CLINTON,

Captain General and Governor in Chief of the Province of New-York, and the Territories thereon depending in AMERICA, *Vice-Admiral of the same, and Vice-Admiral of the Red Squadron of His Majesty's Fleet.*

AND

The Six United *Indian* Nations, and other *Indian* Nations, depending on the PROVINCE of *NEW-YORK.*

Held at *ALBANY* in the Months of *August* and *September,* 1746.

NEW-YORK:
Printed and Sold by *James Parker* at the New-Printing Office in Beaver-Street, 1746.

count of this conference in which he says that Hendrick, a chief of the Mohawks, said to the Eastern Indians: "We, the Mohawks, are your fathers and you are our children. If you are dutiful and obedient, if you brighten the chain with the English our friends and take up the hatchet against the French our enemies, we will defend and protect you; but otherwise if you are disobedient and rebel you shall die every man, woman, and child of you and that by our hands. We will cut you off from this earth as an ox licketh up the grass." It was apparently this promise that the Massachusetts commissioners desired the Mohawks to make good.

The business of the Pennsylvania Commissioners related to the negotiations with the Catawbas (between whom and the Six Nations the Governor of Pennsylvania was trying to make peace) and to some Pennsylvania Indian traders who had been robbed by the Shawanese. The Indian reply to the latter matter was probably not satisfactory.

24

TREATY BETWEEN GOVERNOR CLINTON OF NEW YORK AND THE SIX NATIONS, HELD AT ALBANY IN AUGUST AND SEPTEMBER, 1746.

Printed by Parker at New York in 1746

COLLATION. Folio, pp. 23. Sigs. [A] to F in twos.
SIZE OF LETTERPRESS. 9¾ x 5½.
COPIES LOCATED. NYPL. NYHS. HSP.

SYNOPSIS. There were present Governor George Clinton, Cadwalader Colden, Ph. Livingston, and John Rutherford of the Governor's council, and the Commissioners of Massachusetts and many others and the Indians of the Six Nations. Sir Wm. Johnson, then only Mr. Johnson, was there at the head of the Mohawks. The purpose of the conference was to get the Indians to espouse the side of the English in the war against the French. The hatchet had been given to them the previous year at the Albany conference and they had promised to try to get satisfaction from the Canadian Indians. Now, however, they promised to join in the war.

This Treaty was also reprinted in Colden's "Five Indian Nations of Canada," London, 1747, p. 153.

25

A
TREATY

BETWEEN THE

PRESIDENT *and* COUNCIL

OF THE

Province of PENNSYLVANIA,

AND THE

INDIANS of *OHIO,*

Held at *PHILADELPHIA, Nov.* 13. 1747.

PHILADELPHIA:
Printed and Sold by B. FRANKLIN, at the New
Printing-Office, near the Market.   MDCCXLVIII.

TREATY WITH THE OHIO INDIANS AT PHILADELPHIA IN NOVEMBER, 1747.

Printed by Franklin at Philadelphia, 1748

COLLATION. Folio, pp. 8.
SIZE OF LETTERPRESS. 9⅞ x 5⅜.
COPIES LOCATED. APS. CPC. D. Friend. M. NYPL.

SYNOPSIS. There were present at this treaty the President and Council and a delegation of Indians of the Six Nations from the Ohio country. Conrad Weiser was present as Interpreter.

The Indians came without invitation. They informed the council that at the beginning of the war with France the Six Nations had been advised by the English Colonies to remain neutral but that after the French and some of their Indian allies had attacked the English settlements the Indians had been requested repeatedly to take up the hatchet. That the old men at Onondaga had refused to do this but that "at last the young Indians, the Warriors and Captains consulted together and resolved to take up the English hatchet against the will of their old people and to lay their old people aside as of no use but in time of Peace." This they had done and were now come to ask for more and better weapons with which to carry on their war. They also said that "When once we the young warriors engaged we put a great deal of fire under our kettle and the kettle boiled high and so it does still (meaning they carried on the war briskly) that the Frenchmen's heads might soon be boiled. But when we looked about us to see how it was with the English kettle we saw the fire was almost out and that it hardly boiled at all and that no Frenchmen's heads were like to be in it. This truly surprises us and we are come down on purpose to know the reason of it. How comes it to pass that the English who brought us into the war will not fight themselves? This has not a good appearance and therefore we give you this string of wampum to hearten and encourage you and to desire you would put more fire under your kettle."

They received a plausible answer and a small present and a promise of another present the following year and expressed themselves satisfied.

26

A

TREATY

HELD BY

COMMISSIONERS,

MEMBERS of the COUNCIL of the

PROVINCE of *PENNSYLVANIA*,

At the TOWN of *LANCASTER*,

With some CHIEFS of the *SIX NATIONS* at *OHIO*, and others, for the Admiffion of the TWIGHTWEE NATION into the Alliance of his MAJESTY, &c. in the Month of *July*, 1748.

PHILADELPHIA:

Printed and Sold by B. FRANKLIN, at the New Printing-Office, near the Market. MDCCXLVIII.

TREATY AT LANCASTER BETWEEN THE PROVINCE OF PENNSYLVANIA AND SOME OF THE SIX NATIONS AND THE TWIGHTEES AND SHAWNESE IN JULY, 1748.

Printed by Franklin at Philadelphia, 1748

COLLATION. Small folio. Title and Report 2 ll., pp. 1 to 10. Sigs. [C], D, E and F in twos.
SIZE OF LETTERPRESS. 10 x 5⅜.
COPIES LOCATED. D. NYPL. BM. APS. CPC. M. Friend.

SYNOPSIS. Some of the Six Nations came to intercede for the Twightees and Shawnese who asked to be taken into the friendship of the English. The Twightees described themselves as living on the river Oubache and having twenty towns and one thousand warriors. They were received with satisfaction and a treaty was drawn up to be signed by both parties. The Shawnese on the other hand were reminded that part of their nation had broken the old treaty existing between them and they were taken on probation.

A
JOURNAL
OF THE
PROCEEDINGS
OF THE
COMMISSIONERS
Appointed for Managing
A *Treaty* of *Peace* :

To be Begun and Held at *Falmouth*, in the County of
York, the Twenty-feventh of *September*, Anno Domini
One thoufand feven hundred and forty-nine ;

BETWEEN

Thomas Hutchinfon, *John Choate*, *Ifrael*
Williams, and *James Otis*, Efqrs;

COMMISSIONED by the HONOURABLE

SPENCER PHIPS, Efq;

Lieutenant-Governour and Commander in Chief, in
and over His Majefty's Province of the *Maffachufetts-
Bay* in *New-England*,

on the one Part ;

AND THE

EASTERN INDIANS

on the other Part.

BOSTON ; NEW-ENGLAND : Printed by JOHN DRAPER,
Printer to His Honour the Lieutenant-Governour and Council.

JOURNAL OF THE TREATY MADE AT FALMOUTH IN SEPTEMBER, 1749, BETWEEN MASSACHUSETTS AND THE EASTERN INDIANS

Printed at Boston by Draper

COLLATION. Quarto, pp. 17, [1].
SIZE OF LETTERPRESS. 8¼ x 5⅜.
COPIES LOCATED. LCP. HC. JCB. LC. AAS. MHS.

SYNOPSIS. This treaty began September 29, and ended October 17, 1749. There were present the Commissioners of Massachusetts and the Norridgewock and Penobscot Indians. The principal matters of importance at this peace-making council were in relation to the captives that had been taken on both sides and were to be returned without ransom.

This Treaty was reprinted in Maine Hist. Coll., iv, 145. See also Winsor Nar. and Crit. Hist., V, 450.

28

A

JOURNAL

OF THE

PROCEEDINGS

OF

Jacob Wendell, *Samuel Watts*,
Thomas Hubbard and *Chambers
Russel*, Esq⟨rs⟩;

COMMISSIONERS

appointed by the HONOURABLE

SPENCER PHIPS, Esq;

Lieutenant-Governour and Commander in Chief, in and
over His Majesty's Province of the *Massachusetts-
Bay* in *New-England*,

to Treat with the several Tribes

OF

Eastern Indians,

in order to Renew and Confirm

a general PEACE.

BOSTON in NEW-ENGLAND:

Printed by **John Draper**, Printer to the Honourable the Lieutenant-
GOVERNOUR and COUNCIL. 1752.

JOURNAL OF THE TREATY AT ST. GEORGE'S IN OCTOBER, 1752, BETWEEN MASSACHUSETTS AND THE EASTERN INDIANS.

Printed at Boston by Draper, 1752

COLLATION. Quarto, pp. 16. Sigs. A and B in fours.
SIZE OF LETTERPRESS. $7\frac{1}{2}$ x $4\frac{7}{8}$.
COPIES LOCATED. LCP. N. BPL. JCB. LC. AAS.

SYNOPSIS. The Council began October 13 and ended October 20th, 1752. Present the Commissioners of Massachusetts and the Penobscot and Norridgewock Indians. The object was to renew and confirm a general peace. Governor Dummer's Treaty and the one at Falmouth, 1749, had been broken by the Indians and this council promised amends. There was much discussion about the return of captives taken at Swan Island and North Yarmouth.

See Winsor Nar. and Crit. Hist., V, 450.

TREATY,

O R.

Articles of Peace and Friendſhip renewed, between

Hɪs Exᴄᴇʟʟᴇɴᴄʏ

Peregrine Thomas Hopſon, Eſq;

Captain General and Governor in
Chief, in and over His Majeſty's
Province of *Nova-Scotia* or *Acca-
die*, Vice Admiral of the ſame,
and Colonel of one of His Majeſ-
ty's Regiments of Foot, and His
Majeſty's Council on Behalf of
His Majeſty ;

A N D

Major *Jean Baptiſte Cope*,

Chief Sachem of the *Chiben accadie*
Tribe of *Mickmack* Indians, inhabiting the Eaſtern Coaſt of the
ſaid Province, and *Andrew Hadley Martin, Gabriel Martin,* and
Franciſ Jeremiah, Members and
Delegates of the ſaid Tribe, for
themſelves and their ſaid Tribe,
their Heirs, and the Heirs of their
Heirs forever ; Begun, made and
concluded in the Manner, Form
and Tenor following, *Viz,*

I. T is agreed that the Articles of
Submiſſion and Agreement
made at *Boſton* in *New-England,* by the Delegates of the
Penobſcot, Norridgwolk, and *St. John's* Indians, in the Year 1725, ratified and confirmed by all the *Nova-Scotia* Tribes, at *An-
napolis*

TRAITE,

O U.

Articles de la Paix et de L'Amitié
renouvelleé, Entre

Sᴏɴ Exᴄᴇʟʟᴇɴᴄᴇ

Peregrine Thomas Hopſon, Ecuyer,

Capitaine General et Gouverneur en
Chef, pour le Roy de la *Grande-
Bretagne,* de la Province de la
Nouvelle-Ecoſſe, ou *L'Accadie,*
Vice Amiral de la dite Province,
et Colonel d'un Regiment d'In-
fanterie, et le Conſeil de ſa Majeſté dans cette Province en Fa-
veur de ſa ditte Majeſté d'un Part ;

E T

Le Major *Jean Baptiſte Cope*,

Chef Sachem de la Tribu *Chiben acadia-
ce* des Sauvages *Mickmack,* ha-
bitans les Côtes de l'Eſt de la ditte Province, et *Andre Hadley
Martin, Gabriel Martin,* et Fran-
çois *Jeremie,* Membres et Envoyés
de la ſuſditte Tribu pour eux
memes, leurs Heritiers et les Heritiers de leurs Heritiers a Jamais,
d'une autre Parte ; le dit Traité
commencé, Fait et concluè dans
la Maniere, Forme et Teneur qui
ſ'en ſuivent,

I. N eſt convenu que les Articles
de Soumiſſion et d'Agreément
fait à *Boſton* dans la *Nouvelle-
Angleterre,* par les Sauvages
Deputés de *Penobſcot, Norridgwolk,* et de la
Riviere de *St. Jean,* dans l'Anneé 1725,
ratifié et confirmés par toutes les Tribus de

I2

TREATY BETWEEN GOVERNOR HOPSON AND THE MICMAC INDIANS, IN NOVEMBER, 1752.

Printed at Halifax by John Bushnell, 1753

COLLATION. Folio, pp. 4.
SIZE OF LETTERPRESS. 10¾ x 6½.
COPIES LOCATED. NYHS. NYPL.

SYNOPSIS. This treaty is printed in parallel columns in English and French. There are eight articles. The first article renews former treaties. The second buries the hatchet; the third makes an offensive and defensive alliance; the fourth relates to hunting and fishing privileges and the Indian trade; the fifth and sixth relate to presents of food, blankets, etc., to be given annually to the Indians. The seventh binds the Indians to aid shipwrecked mariners and conduct them to Halifax; and the eighth determines the manner of settling disputes. The Treaty was signed at Halifax, Nov. 22, 1752.

30

A

TREATY

HELD WITH THE

OHIO INDIANS,

AT

CARLISLE,

In OCTOBER, 1753

PHILADELPHIA:

Printed and Sold by B. FRANKLIN, and D. HALL, at the
New-Printing-Office, near the Market. MDCCLIII.

TREATY HELD IN OCTOBER, 1753, AT CARLISLE BETWEEN THE PROVINCE OF PENNSYLVANIA AND THE OHIO INDIANS.

Printed at Philadelphia by Franklin, 1753

COLLATION. Folio, pp. 12.
SIZE OF LETTERPRESS. 12½ x 6½.
COPIES LOCATED. D. LCP. HSP. N. Friend.

SYNOPSIS. There were present for Pennsylvania, Richard Peters, Isaac Norris, and Benj. Franklin. The Indians represented were the Twightees, Shawnese, Wyandots, Delawares, and those of the Six Nations residing on the Ohio. The interpreters were George Croghan, Andrew Montour, and Conrad Weiser.

The Indians had lately held a conference with Virginia at Winchester. They came to ask for assistance against the French who at that time had an expedition in their country. It was this French expedition that Washington met later in the year. The Indians got a few presents and some kind words and were hurried home to protect their frontiers.

A

CONFERENCE

Held at St. *George*'s in the County of *York*,
on the Twentieth Day of *September*, *Anno Regni
Regis* GEORGII *Secundi*, *Magnæ Britanniæ
Franciæ et Hiberniæ*, *Vicesimo Septimo*. Annoque
Domini, 1 7 5 3.

BETWEEN

Sir *William Pepperrell*, Baronet, *Jacob
Wendell*, *Thomas Hubbard*, and *John
Winslow*, Esqrs; and Mr. *James Bowdoin*.

COMMISSIONERS

Appointed by His EXCELLENCY

WILLIAM SHIRLEY, Esq;

Captain General and Governour in Chief, in and over
His Majesty's Province of the *Massachusetts-Bay* in
New-England,

to Treat with the

𝕰𝖆𝖘𝖙𝖊𝖗𝖓 𝕵𝖓𝖉𝖎𝖆𝖓𝖘

of the one Part,
and the 𝕴𝖓𝖉𝖎𝖆𝖓𝖘 of the *Penobscott* Tribe
of the other Part.

BOSTON in *NEW-ENGLAND*:
Printed by 𝖲𝖺𝗆𝗎𝖾𝗅 𝕶𝖓𝖊𝖊𝖑𝖆𝖓𝖉, Printer to the Honourable House of
REPRESENTATIVES. 1 7 5 3.

A CONFERENCE HELD AT ST. GEORGE'S 20TH SEPT., 1753, BETWEEN SIR WM. PEPPERRELL AND OTHERS, THE COMMISSIONERS APPOINTED BY GOV. SHIRLEY, AND THE EASTERN INDIANS.

Printed at Boston, 1753

COLLATION. Quarto, pp. 26.
SIZE OF LETTERPRESS. $7\frac{1}{4}$ x $4\frac{5}{8}$.
COPIES LOCATED. HC. N. JCB. AAS. HEH. MHS.

SYNOPSIS. Like most of the Eastern treaties the principal business of the Indians was to get lower prices for trade articles and of the whites to oppose the French and secure the return of captives. Both of these subjects were much discussed.

See Winsor Nar. and Crit. Hist., V, 450.

32

A

JOURNAL

OF THE

PROCEEDINGS

AT

Two *CONFERENCES*

Begun to be held at *Falmouth* in *Casco-Bay*, in the County
of *York*, within the Province of the *Massachusetts-Bay*
in NEW-ENGLAND, on the Twenty-Eighth Day of *June*
1 7 5 4,

BETWEEN

His EXCELLENCY

WILLIAM SHIRLEY, Esq;

Captain-General, Governour and Commander in Chief, in
and over the Province aforesaid,

And the CHIEFS of the

𝕹𝖔𝖗𝖗𝖎𝖉𝖌𝖜𝖆𝖑𝖐 𝕴𝖓𝖉𝖎𝖆𝖓𝖘;

And on the Fifth Day of *July* following,

Between His said EXCELLENCY

and the CHIEFS of the

𝕻𝖊𝖓𝖔𝖇𝖘𝖈𝖔𝖙 𝕴𝖓𝖉𝖎𝖆𝖓𝖘.

BOSTON in *NEW-ENGLAND* :

Printed by *John Draper*, Printer to His Excellency the
GOVERNOUR and COUNCIL. 1 7 5 4.

JOURNAL OF TWO CONFERENCES BE- TWEEN GOVERNOR SHIRLEY AND THE NORRIDGEWOCKS AND PENOBSCOTS AT FALMOUTH, 1754.

Printed at Boston by Draper, 1754

COLLATION. Folio, pp. 27. Sigs. [A] to G in twos. Sig. A has the first and last leaves.

SIZE OF LETTERPRESS. 10⅜ x 5½.

COPIES LOCATED. LCP. N. LC. HEH.

SYNOPSIS. The meetings were from June 28 to July 6th. The first meetings were with the Norridgewocks. Governor Shirley had come to them at their request instead of sending commissioners. He told them he proposed to build a fort on the Kennebec, to which the Indians objected. There was much talk of the various Indian depre- dations in the past two years and some plain language used on both sides. The Norridgewocks attempted to put the blame of some out- rages on the "Albany" Indians but Governor Shirley gave the names of the leaders showing them to be Eastern Indians. Things were made smooth as they usually were at Indian treaties and a general understanding arrived at.

The Penobscots had agreed to be present but were not there when the Governor arrived. Fearing from a French letter that he had in- tercepted, and which is printed in the treaty minutes, that they were kept away by French influence he sent for them and they finally came and held a friendly council.

The list of outrages committed by the Indians mentioned in the minutes and discussed include Swan Island, Sheeps-cot, Richmond, Brunswick, North Yarmouth, New Meadows, and others.

See Winsor Nar. and Crit. Hist., V, 450.

An ACCOUNT of
CONFERENCES held,
AND
TREATIES made,
Between Major-general
Sir WILLIAM JOHNSON, Bart.
AND
The chief SACHEMS and WARRIOURS
OF THE

Mohawks,	*Skaniadaradighronos,*
Oneidas,	*Chugnuts,*
Onondagas,	*Mahickanders,*
Cayugas,	*Shawanese,*
Senekas,	*Kanuskagos,*
Tuskaroras,	*Toderighronos,* and
Aughquageys,	*Oghquagoes,*

Indian Nations in *North America,*

At their Meetings on different Occasions at *Fort Johnson*
in the County of *Albany,* in the Colony of *New York,*
in the Years 1755 and 1756.

WITH

A Letter from the Rev. Mr. HAWLEY to Sir
WILLIAM JOHNSON, written at the Desire
of the DELAWARE INDIANS.

And a PREFACE

Giving a short Account of the SIX NATIONS, some
Anecdotes of the Life of Sir WILLIAM, and Notes
illustrating the Whole;

Also an APPENDIX

Containing an Account of Conferences between several
Quakers in *Philadelphia,* and some of the Heads of
the *Six Nations,* in *April* 1756.

LONDON:
Printed for A. MILLAR, in the *Strand.* M DCC LVI.
[Price 1s. 6d.]

ACCOUNT OF CONFERENCES HELD AND TREATIES MADE BETWEEN SIR WM. JOHNSON AND VARIOUS TRIBES OF INDIANS IN THE YEAR 1756.

Printed at London, 1756

COLLATION. Octavo, pp. Title verso blank 1 l. pp. xii + [3] to 77.
SIZE OF LETTERPRESS. 6⅜ x 3⅛.
COPIES LOCATED. D. HSP. APS. N. W. JCB. LC. HEH. and others.

SYNOPSIS. This contains a summary of several meetings in the years 1755 and 1756. They relate principally to the war with the Delawares and Shawnese. The first conference was December 7th, 1755, with five of the Six Nations, at which Johnson informs them of the depredations of the Delawares and advises them to put a stop to their barbarities as the Delawares are supposed to be Dependents of the Six Nations.

The next account is December 26. Three tribes of the Six Nations who say they are looking after the River Indians and Shawnese and ask for a fort to protect them from the French. For some reason Johnson's answer to this speech was not given until 17th February, 1756. Then follows a letter from the Rev. Gideon Hawley to Sir William Johnson written at the request of the messengers sent by the Six Nations at Johnson's request to the Delawares. The letter is dated Onhughquagey, December 27th, 1755. It gives the Delaware version of the cause of their taking up the hatchet.

Johnson had called a general Indian Council and it began on February 16th, 1756, although some of the Indians had arrived before and speeches are given as early as February 2nd. At this conference all matters of importance to the Indians and English were discussed. Johnson tells them of the death of Braddock, congratulates them on the success at Lake George and warns the Six Nations that if they do not now exert the authority they claim over the Delawares that they will soon have the latter for enemies instead of friends. This conference extended through the whole month of February. It was

A
TREATY

Between the Government of *New-Jersey*,

AND THE

INDIANS,

Inhabiting the several Parts of said Province,

Held at

CROSWICKS,

In the County of

BURLINGTON

On *Thursday* and *Friday* the *eighth* and *ninth* Day of *January*, 1756.

PHILADELPHIA:
Printed by WILLIAM BRADFORD, Printer to the Province of
New-Jersey.

attended by Rev. Dr. Ogilvie, Rev. Gideon Hawley, Captain Butler and others.

The volume ends with an abstract of the conference between the Quakers and some of the Six Nations at the house of Israel Pemberton at Philadelphia in April, 1756. See No. 37.

See also Winsor Nar. and Crit. Hist., V, 581, and 584.

34

TREATY BETWEEN THE GOVERNOR OF NEW JERSEY AND THE INDIANS OF THAT PROVINCE IN JANUARY, 1756, AT CROSSWICKS.

Printed at Philadelphia by Wm. Bradford

COLLATION. Small folio, pp. 11. Sigs. [A] to C in twos.
SIZE OF LETTERPRESS. 9 x 5⅜.
COPIES LOCATED. NYPL. LCP. APS. M. D.

SYNOPSIS. There were present the Commissioners of New Jersey and the Indians of four tribes, Cranberry, Pompton, Crosswick and South Jersey. The Conference was for the purpose of taking up the complaints on either side. The Indians made their most serious complaint against the sale of rum to the Indians. The Commissioners as usual sympathized with them and did nothing.

35

G:Washington

A

TREATY

HELD WITH THE

CATAWBA and *CHEROKEE* INDIANS,

AT THE

CATAWBA-TOWN *and* BROAD-RIVER

IN THE

Months of *February* and *March* 1756.

By Virtue of a Commission granted by the Honorable
ROBERT DINWIDDIE, Esquire, His Majesty's
Lieutenant-Governor, and Commander in Chief of the Colony
and Dominion of V I R G I N I A, to the Honorable
PETER RANDOLPH and WILLIAM BYRD, Esquires, Members of
His Majesty's Council of the said Colony.

Published by Order of the GOVERNOR.

VIRGINIA
EN · DAT · QUARTAM

WILLIAMSBURG: Printed by W. HUNTER. M,DCC,LVI.

TREATY HELD IN FEBRUARY AND MARCH, 1756, BETWEEN THE GOVERNOR OF VIRGINIA AND THE CATAWBA AND CHEROKEE INDIANS.

Printed at Williamsburg by W. Hunter, 1756

COLLATION. Quarto, pp. xiv, 25. Sigs. A in two, B-E in fours, F in two. SIZE OF LETTERPRESS. 8½ x 5⅝. COPIES SEEN. BA. NYHS.

SYNOPSIS. The treaty with the Catawbas was held at Catawba town, February 20 and 21, 1756, and that with the Cherokees, March 13 to 17, 1756, at Broad River. To both tribes Governor Dunwiddie sent speeches by his Commissioners Peter Randolph and William Byrd. The speeches are printed. The Indians are reproached for some perfidious actions but a treaty is made by which both tribes are to fight against the French.

36

SEVERAL

CONFERENCES

Between some of the principal PEOPLE amongst the

QUAKERS

IN

PENNSYLVANIA,

AND THE

DEPUTIES

FROM THE

SIX INDIAN NATIONS,

In ALLIANCE with BRITAIN;

In order to reclaim their Brethren the DELAWARE INDIANS from their *Defection,* and put a Stop to their *Barbarities* and *Hostilities.*

To which is pr fix'd

(As introductory to the said CONFERENCES)

Two ADDRESSES from the said QUAKERS; one to the Lieutenant-Governor, and the other to the General-Assembly of the Province of *Pennsylvania*; as also the Lieutenant-Governor's DECLARATION of WAR against the said *Delaware Indians,* and their Adherents.

NEWCASTLE UPON TYNE:
Printed by I. THOMPSON and COMPANY.
MDCCLVI.

CONFERENCES BETWEEN SOME QUAKERS AND SOME OF THE SIX NATIONS. IN APRIL, 1756, AT PHILADELPHIA.

Printed at Newcastle upon Tyne in 1756

COLLATION. Octavo, pp. 28.
SIZE OF LETTERPRESS. 6½ x 3⁹⁄₁₆.
COPIES LOCATED. D. BPL. JCB. and others.

SYNOPSIS. Although this is not an official treaty it deserves mention as an attempt to mediate between the Delawares who were on the warpath and the Province of Pennsylvania which had just declared war on them. The conference took place at the house of Israel Pemberton on the 19th, 21st and 23rd, Fourth Month. There were present on the 21st, twenty Quakers, seven Indians and some Indian women and Conrad Weiser, Daniel Claus and Andrew Montour as Interpreters.

The Quakers reminded the Indians of the peaceful conduct of their forefathers and assured them of their good feeling and asked the Indians to find some way to reach the Delawares and persuade them to make peace. The Indians replied that they were glad to know that there were some people left with peaceful principles. "We thought that the people of that profession were all dead or buried in the bushes or in the ashes." They promised to send messengers to the Delawares but advised the Quakers that it would be dangerous for any of them to attempt to go.

An account of this conference is also given in the Account of Conferences with Sir Wm. Johnson printed in London the same year. See No. 34.

The volume also contains addresses to the Lt. Governor and the General Assembly with the Lt. Governor's answer and the Proclamation declaring war on the Delawares.

A

TREATY

WITH THE

Shawanese and Delaware Indians,

Living on and near the Susquehanna River.

NEGOTIATED

At Fort-Johnson, in the County of *Albany*,

IN

The Province of NEW-YORK,

By the Honourable

Sir WILLIAM JOHNSON, Baronet,

His *Majesty's* Sole Agent, and Superintendant of the Affairs of the Six
Confederate Nations of *Indians*, their Allies and Dependents.

(Published from the original Records,)

By Order of His Excellency the Right Honourable

JOHN Earl of LOUDOUN,

Commander in Chief of all His Majesty's Forces in *North-America*, &c. &c.

WITH

A PREFACE,

EXPLAINING

The Rise and Progress of the said TREATY.

NEW-YORK:
Printed and Sold by *J. Parker* and *W. Weyman*, at the *New-Printing-Office* in *Beaver-street*. MDCCLVII.

TREATY WITH THE DELAWARES AND SHAWNESE AT FT. JOHNSON IN JULY, 1756.

Printed at New York by Parker & Weyman, 1757

COLLATION. Folio, pp. 10.
SIZE OF LETTERPRESS. 10⅛ x 5⅜.
COPIES LOCATED. HSP. HC. HLE.

SYNOPSIS. The Preface gives a good summary of Indian affairs for 1755 and 1756. Johnson had held a treaty in February with the Six Nations and asked them to remonstrate with the Delawares and Shawnese who were devastating the frontiers of Pennsylvania. The messengers sent by the Six Nations to these two tribes returned in April with a belt asking Sir William to meet them at Onondaga in May or June at a great Council of the Six Nations. Johnson went to Onondaga in June, but the Delawares and Shawnese did not appear until the Council Fire had been covered, so he invited them to meet him at Ft. Johnson and this folio records the treaty so held.

Sir William as usual was very frank in his speech about the perfidy of the Shawnese and Delawares, but told them he was willing to believe they were bewitched by the French. If they had real grievances he was willing to remove them and if they were willing to cease their depredations he was ready to make a peace. To this the "Delaware King or Chief" [probably Teedyuscung] replied he would inform his people on his return home of what had been said and send an answer. At this Sir William called a meeting of the few chiefs of the Six Nations and told them what he intended to say to the Delawares and asked them to second it. They in turn gave the Delawares a scolding so that the next day the Delaware chief promised to keep his people at Tioga quiet but said he had no control of the Delawares who lived near the French at Ft. Duquesne.

An interesting episode at this treaty was the receipt during the council of the king's patent creating Johnson a baronet and appointing him sole agent of Indian affairs. He showed and explained the patent to the Indians. A Seneca Chief made a congratulatory speech and Sir William furnished a "tub of punch."

38

MINUTES

OF

CONFERENCES,

HELD WITH THE

INDIANS,

A T

EASTON,

In the Months of *July*, and *August*, 1757.

PHILADELPHIA:

Printed and Sold by B. FRANKLIN, and D. HALL, at the
New-Printing-Office, near the Market. MDCCLVII.

MINUTES OF CONFERENCES AT EASTON IN JULY AND NOVEMBER, 1756.

Printed at Philadelphia by Franklin, 1757

COLLATION. Folio, pp. 32.
SIZE OF LETTERPRESS. 12½ x 6½.
COPIES LOCATED. HSP. APS. CPC. JCB.

SYNOPSIS. This is a record of two conferences and two messages to the Indians in an attempt to stop the Indian depredations on the frontiers. The first message refers to the conference in February at Ft. Johnson and the one at the home of Israel Pemberton in April and is dated Phila. April, 1756. The Governor sends a message to the Delawares and Shawnese on the Susquehanna by some of the Indians who were at Pemberton's. He offers peace if they give up their captives.

The second item in the book is the account of a conference at Easton beginning July 28, 1756, with Teedyuscung and fourteen other Delawares. In his speech the Governor recounts the causes of the trouble with the Delawares and Shawnese in great detail and Teedyuscung promised to do all the English asked. The account shows something of the amount of wampum required for a treaty.

The third part of the book is a council at Easton beginning November 8th, with the Delawares and Shawnese. Teedyuscung is again in the lime-light quibbling on his old grievance about land. Captain Newcastle, one of the Sachems of the Six Nations who attended the conference in July, had died in the meantime.

MINUTES

OF

CONFERENCES,

HELD WITH THE

INDIANS,

At HARRIS's FERRY, and at LANCASTER,

In *March*, *April*, and *May*, 1757.

PHILADELPHIA:

Printed and Sold by B. FRANKLIN, and D. HALL, at the *New-Printing-Office*, near the Market. MDCCLVII.

TREATY HELD IN MARCH, APRIL AND MAY, 1757, BETWEEN GEORGE CROGHAN REPRESENTING SIR WM. JOHNSON, AND THE INDIANS AT HARRIS FERRY AND LANCASTER.

Printed at Philadelphia by Franklin, 1757

COLLATION. Large folio, pp. 22. Sigs. [A] to F in twos.
SIZE OF LETTERPRESS. 12½ x 6½.
COPIES LOCATED. NYPL. LCP. HSP. APS. CPC. N. P. M. LC. D. Friend.

SYNOPSIS. These minutes cover two distinct conferences; the first was held at the house of John Harris in April with George Croghan alone of the whites and the second in May at Lancaster at which Governor Denny attended with a large following. At both places there were deputies from all of the Six Nations and also from the Delawares, Nanticokes and Conestogas. The printed account is George Croghan's report to Sir Wm. Johnson of the Minutes kept at the conferences. There is also a report of Conrad Weiser of a journey to Shamokin in April, 1743, on the affairs of Virginia and Maryland.

It was expected that Teedyuscung and his Delaware followers would come to the treaty to settle the complaints he had made the previous year at Easton but although the Indians waited more than a month for him he did not come. He sent various excuses, one of which was a shortage of provisions, on which the Governor sent him a supply but still he did not come. The Mohawks said the Delawares had sent them a haughty speech in which they said they were no longer subject to the Six Nations. It was evident that Teedyuscung did not want to treat with the whites when the Mohawks were present. This appeared later in the year at the treaty at Easton. The conferences were of some interest and importance but the results were small.

See Winsor Nar. and Crit. Hist., V, 596.

PROCEEDINGS

AND

TREATY

WITH

The *Shawanese*, *Nanticokes*, and *Mohikander*

INDIANS,

LIVING

At *Otsiningo*, on one of the West Branches of the
Susquehanna River

NEGOTIATED

At *Fort-Johnson*, in the County of *Albany*, in the Province
of *NEW-YORK*.

BY

The Honourable Sir *William Johnson*, Bart. &c.

PUBLISHED

By Order of his Excellency the Right Honourable

JOHN Earl of LOUDOUN,

Commander in Chief of all His Majesty's Forces in *North-America*, &c.

NEW-YORK:
Printed and Sold by J. PARKER and W. WEYMAN, at the New Printing-Office in
Beaver-Street, MDCCLVII.

CONFERENCE WITH THE MOHICKAN-DERS, SHAWANESE AND NANTICOKES AT FT. JOHNSON, IN APRIL, 1757.

Printed at New York by Parker & Weyman, 1757

COLLATION. Folio, pp. 14. The signature marks are peculiar. Title, verso blank, 1 leaf; pages iii—6, Sig. A in two; pp. 7–10, no mark; pp. 11–14, D in two.

SIZE OF LETTERPRESS. 10⅛ x 5⁷⁄₁₆.

COPIES LOCATED. HLE. LCP. HC. D.

SYNOPSIS. The year 1757 was exceptional for treaties with the Indians. At the same time that this treaty was being held at Ft. Johnson, George Croghan, Sir Wm. Johnson's deputy, was meeting the deputies of these and other Indians at Harris Ferry and Lancaster. These delegates came to Ft. Johnson by an error. In the previous January Sir William had sent a belt to the Shawnese Chief for information and with a request that they would be ready to join the English arms if they should be called upon. The message was understood by them to be an invitation to a council at Ft. Johnson and they came accordingly. Sir William was equal to the occasion and made them welcome and by his good address and diplomacy secured their friendship and sent them home well pleased. The Mohickanders gave him an interesting account of how they happened to be living at Otsiningo on the Susquehanna with the Shawnese and Nanticokes.

The proceedings also give an account of why the Cayugas were not present. They had intended to come with these Indians having been asked by Sir William to come to Ft. Johnson but they had received intelligence from the Oneidas that the latter expected to be attacked by the French and the Cayugas were therefore holding themselves ready to assist the Oneidas.

Sabin, No. 65,759, cites a Boston edition the same year in folio but I have not seen it. Winsor Nar. and Crit. Hist., V, 581 and 596 refers to Sabin but cites no location of the Boston edition.

MINUTES

OF

CONFERENCES,

HELD WITH THE

INDIANS, at *EASTON*,

In the Months of *July* and *November*, 1756;

TOGETHER WITH

Two MESSAGES sent by the GOVERNMENT to the *Indians* residing on *Sasquehannah*; and the REPORT of the COMMITTEE appointed by the ASSEMBLY to attend the GOVERNOR at the last of the said Conferences.

PHILADELPHIA·

Printed and Sold by B. FRANKLIN, and D HALL, at the *New-Printing-Office*, near the Market. MDCCLVII.

TREATY HELD IN AUGUST, 1757, AT EASTON BETWEEN THE PROVINCE OF PENNSYLVANIA AND TEEDYUSCUNG, KING OF THE DELAWARES, REPRESENTING TEN TRIBES OF INDIANS.

Printed at Philadelphia by Franklin, 1757

COLLATION. Large folio, pp. 24. Sigs. [A] to F in twos.
SIZE OF LETTERPRESS. 12½ x 6½.
COPIES LOCATED. D. LCP. HSP. APS. CPC. N. LC. HLE. Friend.

SYNOPSIS. There were present Governor Denny with his Council and many other officials and citizens, Teedyuscung and the representatives of the Ten Nations, i.e. the Six Nations with the Delawares, Shawnese, Nanticokes and Mohicans. George Croghan attended to represent Sir William Johnson and wrote the published report. Thomas McKee, Conrad Weiser and John Pumpshire were the Interpreters.

The Treaty was a most important one, for at it peace was made between the Province of Pennsylvania and the Indians that had for years devastated frontiers. Teedyuscung did most of the talking for the Indians and proved a most difficult person to negotiate with. The fact that the Six Nations had called the Delawares women and forbidden them to sell land still rankled in his mind and he insisted on taking up some of the old land questions which Governor Denny told him had been referred by the Crown to Sir William Johnson to investigate and settle. He objected to going before Sir William whom he said he did not know though he admitted that he was the great friend of the Indians. Evidently he feared to meet there the great men of the Six Nations who would take charge of affairs and relegate him to a back seat. So captious was he that he was finally reproved by another Delaware Chief who said, "What, has not our brother desired you to bring us down by the hand to make Peace? Why don't you do it? We have been here these twenty days and have heard nothing but scolding and disputing about land. Settle the Peace and let all these disputes stand till after." The peace was finally declared, the Indians gave up some of the prisoners they had taken and promised to send in the others.

The official deliberations began on July 25th and ended on August 7th.

See Winsor Nar. and Crit. Hist., V, 596.

A
MESSAGE

FROM

His Excellency FRANCIS BERNARD, Efq;
Captain General Governor and Commander in Chief of *New-Jerfey, &c.*

TO

The *MINISINK INDIANS.*

AND A

CONFERENCE

In Confequence thereof,
Held at *BURLINGTON, Auguft* the 7th and 8th, 1758.

Province of NEW-JERSEY

(**L.S.**) By His Excellency FRANCIS BERNARD, Efq; Captain General, Governor, and Commander in Chief of his Majefty's Colony of *New-Jerfey, &c*

To Teydeuicung, *King of the* Delaware Indians, *by* Mofes Totamy *and* Ifaac Stelle, *Meffengers aeputed by me* ; Greeting.

I WAS furprifed on my Arrival here, with his Majefty's Royal Commiffion, as Governor of this his Province, to find, that Invafions have been lately made on the Inhabitants of this Colony, and much Blood fhed by *Indians,* fuppofed to be thofe of *Minifink* or *Pompton,* who have refided within this Colony, and have fome Time fince withdrawn themfelves · And as I have no Knowledge of any Reafon they, or any of them, have for being difcontented, or offering Violence to the Inhabitants of his Majefty's Colony under my Government , and no publick Complaints have been made by the *Indians* of *Minifink* or *Pompton,* formerly Inhabitants of this Colony, at any of the Conferences held between the Commiffioners of *New-Jerfey,* and the *Indian* Inhabitants of the fame , to prevent any further Hoftilities, I hereby fend you this Power, to go to the *Indians* of *Minifink* and *Pompton,* formerly Inhabitants of this Colony , and in my Name, to defire them to defift from Hoftilities, and kindly to invite them to a Conference with this Colony ; and to affure them that they fhall be received in the moft friendly Manner, and every Endeavour fhall be ufed to eftablifh and confirm a Friendfhip between the Subjects of our Great King GEORGE, our common Father, and them, as a Thing of the greateft Ufe. You are to enforce the natural Affection between us and them, and how much it is for their Intereft to be at Peace with a People, who have the Means of making them happy and eafy, and have, by the Bleffings of Providence, Provifions, and every Neceffary of Life in plenty, fufficient to fupply their Friends in Diftrefs.

As

A MESSAGE FROM HIS EXCELLENCY FRANCIS BERNARD, ESQ., TO THE MINISINK INDIANS. AND A CONFERENCE HELD AT BURLINGTON, AUGUST THE 7TH AND 8TH, 1758.

Philadelphia, 1758

COLLATION. Pp. 6. Caption title.
SIZE OF LETTERPRESS. 10 x 5⅝.
COPY LOCATED. HSP. [The Brinley copy.]

SYNOPSIS. The first item in this paper is a letter from Governor Bernard to Teedyuscung to the effect that depredations on the New Jersey settlers have been committed by the Minisink Indians and the Governor asks him to confer with that tribe and invite them to a conference. This letter which constitutes the "Message" is dated 25 June, 1758.

The conference was attended by the Governor and several members of the Council and the Indians with John Pumpshire as interpreter. After the usual formalities the Indians informed the Governor that they received his overtures for peace with great pleasure and suggested a council at the Forks of the Delaware where the Council Fire was kindled at the next full moon after that date. To this suggestion the Governor agreed.

43

MINUTES

OF

CONFERENCES,

HELD AT

E A S T O N,

In *OCTOBER*, 1758,

With the Chief SACHEMS and WARRIORS of the *Mohawks*, *Oneidoes*, *Qnondagoes*, *Cayugas*, *Senecas*, *Tuscaroras*, *Tuteloes*, *Shaniada-radigronos*, consisting of the *Nanticokes* and *Conoys*, who now make one Nation, *Chugnuts*, *Delawares*, *Unamies*, *Mabickanders*, or *Mobickons*; *Minisinks*, and *Wapingers*, or *Pumptons*.

PHILADELPHIA:

Printed and Sold by B. FRANKLIN, and D. HALL, at the *New-Printing-Office*, near the Market. MDCCLVIII.

CONFERENCE AT EASTON IN OCTOBER, 1758, BETWEEN THE GOVERNORS OF PENNSYLVANIA AND NEW JERSEY AND INDIANS OF THE SIX NATIONS, DELAWARES, MINNISINKS AND MANY OTHER TRIBES.

Printed at Philadelphia by Franklin, 1758

COLLATION. Large folio, pp. 31. Sigs. [A] to H in twos.
SIZE OF LETTERPRESS. 12½ x 6½.
COPIES LOCATED. D. HSP. APS. CPC. N. P. JCB. M. LC.

SYNOPSIS. Present, Governors Denny and Bernard with their Commissioners and others. George Croghan, Deputy agent under Sir Wm. Johnson, 507 Indians representing fifteen tribes and Conrad Weiser, Henry Montour, Stephen Calvin, Isaac Stille and Moses Tittany, Interpreters. This conference was held to settle many things left undone at the Treaty made at Easton in 1757. At that treaty Teedyuscung, the Delaware chief, had been the chief man and done all the talking for the Indians but now the great chiefs of the Six Nations were present and one of the first questions they asked was "Who made Teedyuscung a great man and wherefore is he called a King?" He was careful at this Conference to call the Six Nations "Uncles" and they treated him with scant courtesy. He had promised the previous year to return all the captives he had, which he had not done. One of the Oneida Chiefs rebuked him saying: "Remember, cousin, you have made this promise in our presence. You did it indeed before and you ought to have performed it. It is a shame for one who calls himself a great man to tell Lies," with much more to the same effect.

Many land matters were taken up and the government of Pennsylvania agreed to renounce its claim to part of the land it had bought at Albany three years before and deed it back to the Indians. New Jersey also settled the claim of the Minnisinks for all the land they claimed in New Jersey.

THE
MINUTES
OF A
TREATY

HELD AT

EASTON, in *Pennsylvania*,
In October, 1758.

BY

The Lieutenant Governor of PENNSYLVANIA,

AND

The Governor of NEW-JERSEY;

WITH

The Chief Sachems and Warriors of the

MOHAWKS,	NANTICOKES and CONOYS,
ONEYDOS,	CHUGNUTS,
ONONDAGAS,	DELAWARES,
CAYUGAS,	UNAMIES,
SENECAS,	MOHICKONS,
TUSCARORAS,	MINISINKS, and,
TUTELOES,	WAPINGS.

Woodbridge, in *New-Jersey*:
Printed and Sold by *James Parker*, Printer to the Government of
New-Jersey, 1758.

One of the events of the Conference was the arrival of the messengers who had accompanied Christian Frederick Post on his journey to Ohio. They reported a message from the Ohio Indians and an answer was sent in return.

This Treaty appears with the date 1759 on the title in the LCP, HLE, and Friends copies.

CONFERENCE AT EASTON IN OCTOBER, 1758.

Reprinted at Woodbridge, New Jersey, by James Parker, 1758

COLLATION. Folio, pp. 35.
SIZE OF LETTERPRESS. 10 x 5½.
COPIES LOCATED. NYHS. NJ.

MINUTES

OF

CONFERENCES,

HELD AT

E A S T O N,

In *AUGUST*, 1761.

With the Chief SACHEMS and WARRIORS of the

ONONDAGOES,		*CAYUGAS,*
ONEIDAS,		*NANTICOKES,*
MOHICKONS,		*DELAWARES,*
TUTELOES,		*CONOYS.*

PHILADELPHIA:
Printed and Sold by B. FRANKLIN, and D. HALL, at the
New-Printing-Office, near the Market. MDCCLXI.

MINUTES OF CONFERENCE IN AUGUST, 1761, AT EASTON, WITH ONONDAGAS, CAYUGAS, ONEIDAS, NANTICOKES, MOHICANS, DELAWARES, TUTELOES AND CONOYS.

Printed at Philadelphia by Franklin, 1761

COLLATION. Folio, pp. 18. Sigs. [A] to E in twos.
SIZE OF LETTERPRESS. 12⅝ x 6½.
COPIES LOCATED. LCP. HSP. CPC. BPL. P. D.

SYNOPSIS. Present Lt. Gov. James Hamilton and others with representatives of the eight tribes to the amount of nearly 500. Samuel Weiser, James Sherlock, Joseph Pepy, Interpreters. The conference began August 3rd and ended August 12th. The business of the treaty consisted largely of questions about law and captives. Teedyuscung was there again trying to open up questions that he himself had settled at previous treaties. The question of the settlement made by the Connecticut claimants at Wyoming was discussed. The Indians were requested to annul the sale of any lands they had sold to Connecticut settlers. The Cayugas said they had given to Sir Wm. Johnson all the white captives of their tribe, but the Delawares and others had not complied with their promise made at Easton in 1758 to do so.

46

MINUTES

OF

CONFERENCES,

HELD AT

LANCASTER,

In *AUGUST,* 1762.

With the SACHEMS and WARRIORS of several Tribes of

Northern and *Western* INDIANS.

PHILADELPHIA:

Printed and Sold by B. F R A N K L I N, and D. H A L L, at the
New-Printing-Office, near the Market. MDCCLXIII.

MINUTES OF CONFERENCES AT LANCASTER IN AUGUST, 1762, WITH NORTHERN AND WESTERN INDIANS.

Printed at Philadelphia by Franklin, 1763

COLLATION. Folio, pp. 36. Sigs. [A] to G in twos.
SIZE OF LETTERPRESS. 12¾ x 6½.
COPIES LOCATED. LCP. HSP. APS. CPC. P. HEH. D. Friend.

SYNOPSIS. The conference began August 11th and ended August 28th. Present Lt. Gov. James Hamilton and others with representatives of the Delawares, Shawnese, Twightees, Wawachtanies, Tuscaroras and Kickapos. Isaac Stille and Frederick Post Interpreters. These were all from the Ohio country or the West. On the 14th representatives of the Senecas, Onondagas, Cayugas, Oneidas and Conoys attended. The affairs of this conference were most interesting from the fact that many captives were brought to the meeting to be given up and as the names of these captives are given as well as their captors and the localities where they were taken, the printed minutes take on an interest that is lacking in some printed treaties.

The Connecticut claims to land at Wyoming were discussed and the Indians said that Connecticut had paid some Indians $2,000.00 for this land but that the sale had never been discussed in the Councils of the Six Nations and was therefore void.

Teedyuscung was again in evidence and his affairs were finally disposed of.

47

JOURNAL

OF THE

CONGRESS

OF THE FOUR

SOUTHERN GOVERNORS,

AND THE

SUPERINTENDENT OF THAT DISTRICT,

WITH THE

FIVE NATIONS OF INDIANS,

AT AUGUSTA, 1763.

SOUTH-CAROLINA:
CHARLES-TOWN: Printed by PETER TIMOTHY, M,DCC,LXIV.

JOURNAL OF THE CONGRESS OF THE FOUR SOUTHERN GOVERNORS . . . WITH THE FIVE [SOUTHERN] NATIONS OF INDIANS AT AUGUSTA IN NOVEMBER, 1763.

COLLATION. Folio, pp. [4] + 3 to 45.
SIZE OF LETTERPRESS. 11½ x 5⅜.
COPY LOCATED. W. J. DeRenne.

SYNOPSIS. The first twenty-one pages are taken up with the correspondence and deliberations over the place of holding the treaty, Augusta being finally determined upon. The Congress was finally opened November 5 with Governors Wright of Georgia, Boone of South Carolina, Dobbs of North Carolina, and Lt. Gov. Fauquier and Superintendent John Stuart representing the Southern Colonies and about 700 Indians of the Cherokees, Choctaws, Chickasaws, Creeks and Catawbas. The Interpreters were John Butler, James Beamer, John Watts, James Colbert, Stephen Forrest and John Proctor. Governor Wright opened the conference and made Superintendent Stuart spokesman for the whites. The minutes of the proceedings and reports of the various speeches occupy pages 21 to 38, in which much friendship is professed on both sides, one Indian saying they were "as good friends as if they had sucked one breast." He thought the Traders made all the trouble and thought their number should be limited to two.

Pages 38–41 record the Treaty agreed upon. The white people were to be secure. The Indians forgiven past offenses. They were to live together as one people. The Traders were to be protected. Justice was to rule and all murderers were to be executed. And the Boundaries occupied by the various tribes and the Whites were defined. The remainder is devoted to correspondence about the treaty in which is expressed distrust in the good faith of the Creeks. Fifty copies of the Treaty were ordered printed. The Conference was a very important one and the foregoing gives no idea of the details of the grievances of both sides that were discussed.

V I E W

OF THE

T I T L E

TO

I N D I A N A,

A TRACT OF COUNTRY

ON THE

R I V E R   O H I O.

C O N T A I N I N G

INDIAN CONFERENCES at *Johnson-Hall,* in *May,* 1765---the DEED of the *Six Nations* to the Proprietors of *Indiana*---the MINUTES of the Congress at Fort *Stanwix,* in *October* and *November,* 1768---the DEED of the *Indians,* settling the Boundary Line between the *English* and *Indians* Lands---and the OPINION of Counsel on the Title of the Proprietors of *Indiana.*

P H I L A D E L P H I A:

Printed by S T Y N E R and C I S T, in *Second-street,* near *Arch-street.* M DCC LXXVI.

VIEW OF THE TITLE TO INDIANA

Printed at Philadelphia, 1776

COLLATION. Octavo, pp. 46.

SIZE OF LETTERPRESS.

COPIES LOCATED. LC. HEH. AAS. H. R. Wagner.

It is said that it was also issued without imprint and date but I have not seen such a copy.

SYNOPSIS. In the spring of 1763, a number of Traders were plundered by the Shawnese, Delawares and others of the Ohio River Indians of goods and furs to the value as was claimed of £80,000. They represented their case to Sir Wm. Johnson, who laid it before the Indians at the councils held at Ft. Johnson in 1765 and 1768. At the latter the Indians agreed to give the traders a tract of land south of the Ohio, and bordering on it and on the Monongahela in payment. This grant by the Indians was not confirmed by the King in 1770 when he ratified the treaty of 1768 establishing a boundary line but the case was reserved for later consideration.

To more effectually prosecute their claims the traders gave power of attorney to William Trent and during the negotiations and lobbying necessary in London to get it allowed it became known as the "Case of Wm. Trent."

Probably the first publication to contain these treaties is the "Case." It is a quarto 10½ inches by 8¼ with 8 pp. giving a résumé of the traders' case, and 24 pp. of Appendix which prints the Minutes of the two treaties and the Indians deeds. This quarto I have seen only in the New York Public Library, and that copy shows no evidence of ever having had a title page; the only title is the caption to the first leaf, CASE. It was probably printed in London about 1770. The Appendix of the "Case" is the same as the "View of the Title to Indiana" except that in the latter the legal opinions of Dagge and others have been added.

This same subject is discussed in "Report of the Lords Commissioners for Trade and Plantations on the Petition . . . for a Grant of Land on the River Ohio," etc. Lond. 1772. The treaties were again reprinted in "Plain Facts: being an Examination into the

MINUTES

OF

CONFERENCES,

HELD AT

FORT-PITT,

In APRIL and MAY, 1768,

UNDER THE DIRECTION OF

GEORGE CROGHAN, Esquire,

DEPUTY AGENT for *INDIAN* AFFAIRS,

WITH THE

CHIEFS and WARRIORS

OF THE

Ohio and other *Western* INDIANS.

PHILADELPHIA:

Printed and Sold by WILLIAM GODDARD, at the *New Printing-Office,* in *Market-Street.*

Rights of the Indian Nations of America to their respective Countries," etc. Phila. 1781, said to be by Samuel Wharton. Wharton and Franklin were both interested in pressing the Claim at London and it is not improbable that some of the tracts relating to it were written by them. The whole case became a great land scheme which was finally combined with others and was known then as The "Walpole Company."

49

MINUTES OF CONFERENCE AT FT. PITT IN APRIL AND MAY, 1768.

Printed at Philadelphia by Hall, 1769

COLLATION. Folio, pp. 22. Sigs. [A] to F in twos.
SIZE OF LETTERPRESS. 12½ x 6⅜.
COPIES LOCATED. LCP. HSP.

SYNOPSIS. This conference was between George Croghan, Deputy Agent for Indian Affairs, and Indians of the Six Nations, Delawares, Shawnese, Munseys and Mohicans. Over 1100 Indians attended. Henry Montour was Interpreter.

The murders of Indians and whites was the first business and a list of them is given. A Shawnese Chief accused the whites of holding forts in the Ohio country against the wishes of the Indians but he was reproved by a speaker of the Six Nations who said that it was agreed that when the French were driven out the English should hold their forts. The alleged treaty of Col. Bradstreet with the Indians in 1764 was produced to confound the Shawnese in their contention.

One of the interesting cases considered was a settlement made at Redstone Creek by some Pennsylvanians. They were ordered to leave by the Governor but the Indians objected and asked them to remain.

50